This book is due for return on or before the last date shown below.

Meno
for th
MRCO
and B

Menopause for the MRCOG and beyond

Margaret Rees
MA, DPhil, FRCOG

Honorary Senior Clinical Lecturer in Obstetrics and Gynaecology,
Women's Centre, John Radcliffe Hospital, Oxford, OX3 9DU

Series Editor: David Sturdee

RCOG Press

Published by the **RCOG Press** at
The Royal College of Obstetricians and Gynaecologists
27 Sussex Place, Regent's Park
London NW1 4RG

Registered charity no. 213280

Cover illustration: Osteoporotic bone-scanning electron micrograph, Professor Alan Boyde, Dept of Anatomy and Developmental Biology, University College London; reproduced by permission of the Wellcome Trust Medical Photographic Library.

RCOG Editor: Sophie Leighton
Printed by Cromwell Press Ltd.

Acknowledgements

Figure 1.1: is adapted from 'The menopausal transition: analysis of LH, FSH, estradiol, and progesterone concentrations during menstrual cycles of older women', by Sherman, B.M., West, J.H. and Korenman, S.G., *Journal of Clinical Endocrinology and Metabolism*, 1976, 42: 629–36 by permission of the Endocrine Society. Figure 2.1 and Table 6.1 are reproduced from Rees, M. and Purdie, D.W. *Management of the Menopause*, 1999, by permission of British Menopause Society Publications. Figure 2.2 is reproduced from Riggs, B.L. and Melton, L.J., 'Involutional osteoporosis', *New England Journal of Medicine*, 314: 1676–86 by permission of the Massachusetts Medical Society. Figure 2.3 is adapted from 'Consequences of hip fracture after one year' by Sernbo, I. and Johnell, O., *Osteoporosis International* 1993, 3: 148–53, by permission of *Osteoporosis International*. Figure 6.2 is reproduced from 'The new science of hormone replacement therapy', by Dey, M., *Journal of the British Menopause Society*, Supplement S2, 1999, p. 4, by permission of British Menopause Society Publications and Wyeth UK. Table 1.1 is reproduced with thanks to the Pennell Initiative for Women's Health and Table 5.1 is adapted with permission from Elsevier Science.

Contents

Preface

Until relatively recently, the management of the menopause and hormone replacement therapy (HRT) would not have featured heavily in the MRCOG examinations. Now every candidate must be prepared for the subject to appear in any, or possibly even all, of the different elements of the examination. Over the last few years there has been a rapid expansion in the numbers of HRT preparations, regimens and routes of administration, together with important research findings on the merits and risks of HRT, so this presents a broad and interesting subject that impinges on many aspects of gynaecological care.

Starting with definitions and physiology, the author goes on to discuss the consequences of ovarian failure, the benefits and risks of HRT, its preparations and how to monitor them and the relation to specific pre-existing medical conditions. Consideration is also given to non-hormone replacement therapy and osteoporosis and to the role of complementary and alternative therapies.

The modern gynaecological patient is much more aware and knowledgeable about the menopause and the therapeutic options, with information that is obtained from a variety of sources. Some of this information is unscientific, and many so-called remedies are unproven. The modern gynaecologist therefore needs to have confidence in being able to discuss, evaluate and manage women with menopausal problems. This review, which is aimed at the MRCOG trainee, provides an excellent insight with more than enough current facts and figures, but it will also be most useful for anyone else wishing to be up-to-date in this increasingly important area.

David Sturdee
December 2001

1 Introduction, definitions and physiology

The management of the menopausal woman is an area where the gynaecologist also becomes a physician, dealing with the consequences not only of ovarian failure but also of ageing. The menopause affects many organ systems, and a holistic approach needs to be taken.

Overall, the median age of menopause is 51 years and this has not changed significantly since early Greek times. However, it occurs earlier in smokers than in non-smokers. The age of menopause may be determined *in utero*, with growth restriction in late gestation and low weight gain in infancy leading to an earlier menopause. It also occurs earlier in women with Down syndrome.

Worldwide there has been a significant increase in life expectancy, with a marked expansion of the elderly population, in which women form the majority of the oldest old. Appreciating the problems of older people, the United Nations General Assembly designated 1999 as 'The International Year of Older Persons'. In the UK average female life expectancy is currently 80 years. Thus British women can expect to enjoy about 30 years of postmenopausal life. Since an increasing number of women will live until the age of 100, the menopause can now be considered to be a mid-life stage. In 1996 it was estimated that there were 12 216 000 women (see Table 1.1) and 10 397 000 men aged over 45 years.

Table 1.1	United Kingdom population - women aged 45–85+ (000s)		
Age band	1991	1996	2001
45–59	4769	5303	5624
60–64	1498	1415	1455
65–74	2795	2743	2601
75–84	1968	1945	1976
85+	682	810	898
Total	11 730	12 216	12 554

Adapted from Table 1, the Pennell Report, 1998.

Definitions

Various definitions are current, which are detailed below:

- Menopause

Menopause is the permanent cessation of menstruation resulting from loss of ovarian follicular activity. Natural menopause is recognised to have occurred after 12 consecutive months of amenorrhoea, for which there is no other obvious pathological or physiological cause. Menopause occurs with the final menstrual period, which is known with certainty only in retrospect a year or more after the event. No adequate biological marker exists.

- Perimenopause

This includes the period beginning with the first clinical, biological and endocrinological features of the approaching menopause (e.g. vasomotor symptoms, menstrual irregularity) and ending 12 months after the last menstrual period.

- Menopausal transition

Menopausal transition is that period of time before the final menstrual period when variability in the menstrual cycle is usually increased.

- Climacteric

This is the phase in the ageing of women marking the transition from the reproductive to the non-reproductive state.

- Climacteric syndrome

The climacteric is sometimes but not always associated with symptomatology. When this occurs, the term 'climacteric syndrome' may be used.

- Premenopause

This term is often used ambiguously to refer to one or two years immediately before the menopause, or to the whole of the reproductive period prior to the menopause. Currently it is recommended that this term be used in the latter sense to encompass the entire reproductive period up to the final menstrual period.

- Postmenopause

This should be defined as dating from the final menstrual period, regardless of whether the menopause was induced or spontaneous. However, it cannot be determined until after a period of 12 months of spontaneous amenorrhoea has been observed.

● Premature menopause

Ideally, premature menopause should be defined as menopause that occurs at an age less than two standard deviations below the mean estimated for the reference population. In practice, in the absence of reliable estimates of the distribution of age of natural menopause in developing countries, the age of 40 years is frequently used as an arbitrary cut-off point, below which the menopause is said to be premature.

● Induced menopause

This is defined as the cessation of menstruation that follows either surgical removal of both ovaries or iatrogenic ablation of ovarian function (e.g. by chemotherapy or radiotherapy).

Ovarian function

The menopause is caused by ovarian failure. The ovary has a finite endowment of germ cells with a maximum number of 7 million ovarian follicles at 20 weeks of fetal life. From mid-gestation onwards there is a logarithmic reduction in germ cells until the oocyte store becomes exhausted, on average at the age of 51 years. Fewer than 0.5% are ovulated and follicles are lost through atresia or apoptosis. This results in a fall in production of oestradiol and inhibin and an increase in gonadotrophin levels. The ovary gradually becomes less responsive to gonadotrophins several years before the final menstrual period. Thus there is a gradual increase in circulating levels of follicle-stimulating hormone (FSH) and later luteinising hormone (LH), and a decrease in oestradiol and

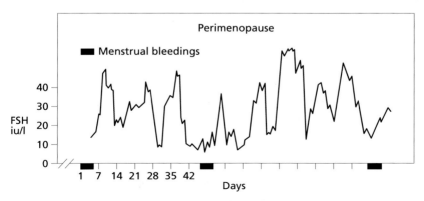

Figure 1.1 Fluctuations in hormone levels in the perimenopause

inhibin levels. FSH levels fluctuate markedly from premenopausal to postmenopausal values, virtually on a daily basis during the menopausal transition. These changes in circulating hormone levels frequently occur in the face of ovulatory menstrual cycles. As ovarian unresponsiveness becomes more marked, cycles tend to become anovulatory. Complete failure of follicular development eventually occurs and oestradiol production is no longer sufficient to stimulate the endometrium; amenorrhoea follows and FSH and LH levels become persistently elevated. FSH levels greater than 30iu/l are generally considered to be in the postmenopausal range. See Figure 1.1.

Premature ovarian failure

Women with premature ovarian failure are at increased risk of developing osteoporosis and cardiovascular disease. In the absence of oophorectomy premature ovarian failure could be more appropriately called premature ovarian dysfunction since spontaneous return of ovarian activity may occur, leading to pregnancy.

PRIMARY PREMATURE OVARIAN FAILURE

Primary premature ovarian failure can occur at any age, even in teenagers. It can present as either primary or secondary amenorrhoea. In the vast majority of cases no cause can be found. The causes are detailed below.

- Chromosome abnormalities

  Chromosome abnormalities, particularly of the X chromosome, have been implicated. X-chromosome mosaicisms are the most common abnormality in women with premature ovarian failure. In Turner syndrome (45XO), accelerated follicular loss causes ovarian failure. Familial premature ovarian failure has been linked with fragile X permutations. Women with Down syndrome also have an early menopause.

- Autoimmune disease

  Autoimmune endocrine disease such as hypothyroidism, Addison's disease and diabetes may be associated with premature ovarian failure.

- FSH receptor abnormalities

  Mutations of gonadotrophin receptors have been reported.

- Disruption of oestrogen synthesis

  Specific enzyme deficiencies (e.g. 17-alpha-hydroxylase) can prevent oestradiol synthesis, leading to primary amenorrhoea and elevated gonadotrophin levels despite the presence of developing follicles.

● Metabolic galactosaemia

Galactosaemia is associated with premature ovarian failure. It is thought that galactose and its metabolites may be toxic to the ovarian parenchyma.

CAUSES OF PREMATURE OVARIAN FAILURE

Primary	Secondary
Chromosome abnormalities	Bilateral oophorectomy or surgical menopause
Autoimmune disease	
FSH receptor abnormalities	Hysterectomy without oophorectomy
Disruption of oestrogen synthesis	Radiotherapy and chemotherapy
Metabolic galactosaemia	Infection

SECONDARY PREMATURE OVARIAN FAILURE

This is becoming more important as survival rates following the treatment of malignancy continue to improve. However, the development of techniques to conserve ovarian tissue/oocytes before therapy is instigated should help at least with maintaining fertility. The causes of secondary premature ovarian failure are detailed below.

● Bilateral oophorectomy or surgical menopause

This results in immediate menopause symptoms, such as hot flushes and night sweats. The implications of this procedure require detailed discussion with the patient in view of the increased morbidity and mortality in those who do not take oestrogen replacement.

● Hysterectomy without oophorectomy

This can cause ovarian failure either in the immediate postoperative period, where in some cases it may be temporary, or at a later stage that is earlier than the usual age of menopause. This is an area of controversy and may depend on ovarian function preceding hysterectomy. The diagnosis may be difficult, since not all women suffer acute symptoms, and in the absence of a uterus the pointer of amenorrhoea is absent. A case could be made for annual FSH estimation in women who have had a hysterectomy before the age of 40 years.

- Radiotherapy and chemotherapy

  Chemotherapy can cause either temporary or permanent ovarian damage, which depends on the cumulative dose received and duration of treatment, so that long-term treatment with small doses is more toxic than short-term acute therapy. These changes occur at all ages, but especially in women of more than 30 years of age. With regard to radiotherapy, ovarian damage is dose- and age-dependent.

- Infection may in rare cases affect the ovaries

  Tuberculosis and mumps are infections that have been implicated. In most cases normal ovarian function occurs after mumps infection.

Reference

Pennell Report on Women's Health (1998). The Pennell Initiative, Health Services Management Unit, University of Manchester, Devonshire House, Precinct Centre, Oxford Road, Manchester, M13 9PL.

2 Consequences of ovarian failure

Short-term consequences

The short-term consequences associated with the menopause are vasomotor symptoms, mood disorders, urogenital and sexual changes. There appear to be cultural differences in attitudes to the menopause; for example, menopausal complaints are fewer in Japanese and Chinese than in North American women. For example, while about 70% of women in western cultures experience vasomotor symptoms, only 18% of Chinese women do so. Furthermore, a recent Swedish study (Stadberg *et al.* 2000) showed that women with a higher level of education and women who exercised regularly were more often symptom-free.

VASOMOTOR SYMPTOMS

Hot flushes and night sweats are episodes of inappropriate heat loss. Sympathetic nervous control of skin blood flow is impaired in women with menopausal flushes, in that reflex constriction to an ice stimulus cannot be elicited. Hot flushes can occur at any time and at night disturb sleep. Chronically disturbed sleep can in turn lead to insomnia, irritability and difficulties with short-term memory and concentration. The prevalence of vasomotor symptoms is highest in the first year after the final menstrual period.

MOOD DISORDERS

The mood disorders that have been associated with the menopause include depression, anxiety, irritability, mood swings, lethargy and lack of energy. However, general population studies suggest that the majority of women do not experience major mood changes during the menopause transition. Studies of depressive symptoms in menopausal women indicate that menopause is not associated with increased rates of depression, although mild mood and anxiety symptoms may occur in the few years prior to menopause. Women with previous affective disorders that are cyclic or that are associated with reproductive events may be at increased risk for depression at menopause.

It is also important to take account of other factors that are present generally in the life of the menopausal woman. In the past, emphasis has been on a woman's change of role, resulting for example from the 'empty nest'. With increased longevity, problems with ageing parents may also contribute. Bereavement, marital difficulties, work and economic problems must also be taken into account.

UROGENITAL ATROPHY

Embryologically the female genital tract and urinary systems develop in close proximity, both arising from the primitive urogenital sinus. Animal and human studies have shown that the urethra is oestrogen-sensitive, and oestrogen receptors have been identified in the human female urethra, urinary bladder, the vagina and the pelvic floor muscles. Urogenital complaints such as vaginal discomfort, dysuria, dyspareunia, recurrent lower urinary tract infections and urinary incontinence are more common in women after the menopause. Epidemiological studies have demonstrated that more than 50% of postmenopausal women suffer from at least one of these symptoms. Symptoms not only cause discomfort for the afflicted individual but may also negatively influence sexual health.

Several features of the vaginal micro-environment change with increasing age, mostly in response to alterations in oestrogen and progesterone concentrations. The histology of the vagina changes extensively after the menopause, when the mucosa often becomes quite thin, and heavily infiltrated with neutrophils. The hormonal changes associated with the menopause have also been shown to induce changes in the bacterial colonisation of the vagina. After the menopause the vagina is colonised with a predominantly faecal flora in contrast to the dominance with lactobacilli premenopausally. The presence of lactobacilli provides protection against vaginal and periurethral colonisation by Gram-negative bacteria, which have been implicated in the pathogenesis of cystitis and urethritis.

SEXUAL CHANGES

A common complaint in menopausal women is vaginal dryness leading to dyspareunia and lack of libido. Changes in sexual behaviour and activity are not uncommon in menopausal women. It is relevant that few studies have considered the effects of menopause on sexuality. Large studies with representative samples using postal questionnaires have included only a few sexual variables. More comprehensive studies have tended to employ non-representative samples. Evidence from existing research suggests a decline in sexual interest, frequency of sexual intercourse and vaginal lubrication in association with the menopause. Findings for variables such as capacity for orgasm, satisfaction with the sexual partner and vaginal pain or discomfort are few and mixed. Other factors, such as conflict between partners, insomnia, inadequate stimulation, life stress or depression are important contributors to a woman's level of interest in sexual activity. In addition, male sexual problems, for example loss of libido and erectile difficulties, should not be ignored.

Long-term consequences of the menopause

With increased longevity the long-term complications of the menopause are likely to have a greater impact on a woman's quality life than the acute short-term symptoms. The long-term complications of greatest interest are osteoporosis, cardiovascular disease and urogenital atrophy. Table 2.1 lists the causes of death in women aged over 50 years in England and Wales.

Table 2.1 Causes of death in women over the age of 50 years in England and Wales 1999. ONS 2000

Cause of death	ICD(9) code	Deaths (n)
Ischaemic heart disease	410–414	51 366
Stroke	430–438	34 821
Breast cancer	174	10 276
Colon cancer	153	4 953
Endometrial cancer	182.0	775
Osteoporosis	733.0	998
Alzheimer's disease	331.0	1 694
Venous thromboembolism	451–453	1 022
Road traffic accidents	E810–E819	412
All deaths		279 856

OSTEOPOROSIS

Osteoporosis is often called the 'silent disease' because bone loss occurs without symptoms, and the first sign is a fracture following minor trauma. Osteoporosis has been defined by the World Health Organization as *a disease characterised by low bone mass and micro-architectural deterioration of bone tissue, leading to enhanced bone fragility and a consequent increase in fracture risk.* It is estimated to affect 75 million people in the USA, Europe and Japan combined and affects one in three postmenopausal women.

The difference between osteoporosis (insufficient bone) and osteomalacia (inadequately mineralised bone) was established by Pommer in 1885. In the

1930s it became recognised as the cause of vertebral crush fractures in oophorectomised women.

Osteoporosis is a feature of both elderly men and women, but in general elderly men have fewer fractures than women. The age-related increase in fracture begins earlier in women, partly because they experience more bone loss and fall more than men. In addition there may be some biomechanical factors, such as relatively larger bone size, that offer men some protection against fractures. There is an ethnic variation in the susceptibility to osteoporosis with, for example, Caucasian women having a higher rate of fracture than those of Afro-Caribbean origin. It is unlikely that there is a single gene defect for osteoporosis, but several possible ones have been examined, including those for the vitamin D receptor, oestrogen receptor and collagen.

LIFETIME CHANGES OF BONE DENSITY

Bone density increases during childhood and adolescence, reaching a peak during the third decade when it plateaus. A higher peak bone mass is reached in men compared with women. Peak bone density is then sustained for some years and begins to decline sometime during the mid-40s. Following the menopause there is an accelerated period of bone loss, which lasts for six to ten years, and which does not occur in men.

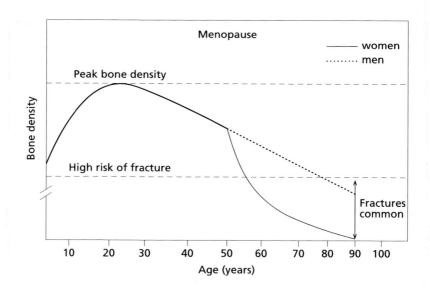

Figure 2.1 Lifetime changes of bone density

Thereafter bone loss continues but at a much slower rate (Figure 2.1). The development of osteoporosis depends on the peak bone density attained and subsequent bone loss. Intuitively some of the preventive measures for osteoporosis are to encourage a good diet rich in calcium and vitamin D and weight-bearing exercise, and discourage smoking in adolescence. However, studies regarding the efficacy of these interventions are required.

FRACTURES

Fractures of the wrist (Colles), hip and vertebrae, which are the main clinical manifestations of osteoporosis, have enormous impact on quality of life, result in significant economic burden and, particularly in the case of hip fractures, are associated with considerable excess mortality. By the age of 80 years, the majority of women will have sustained one or more fractures of varying severity. As an order of magnitude annual NHS expenditure on the acute and aftercare of osteoporosis-related fracture is close to £1 billion.

Colles fractures

These often occur following a fall on an outstretched hand. Although such fractures seldom require hospitalisation, they are painful and considerably reduce mobility and function.

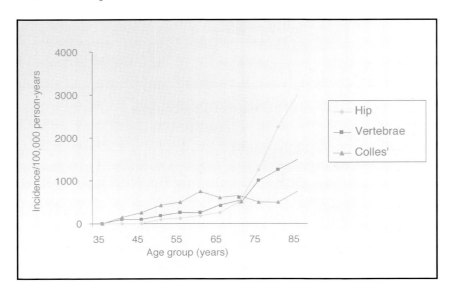

Figure 2.2 Incidence of spine, hip and wrist fractures with age

Hip fractures

These are caused by falls or may even occur spontaneously. The incidence rate of hip fracture is approximately twice as high in women as in men. In many western countries the remaining lifetime risk of a hip fracture in Caucasian women at the age of menopause is approximately 14%. Hip fracture is associated with more deaths, disability and medical costs than all other osteoporotic fractures combined. In the year following a hip fracture, the mortality rate is approximately 20% higher in patients than in controls. Patients who do survive hip fracture often suffer permanent disability.

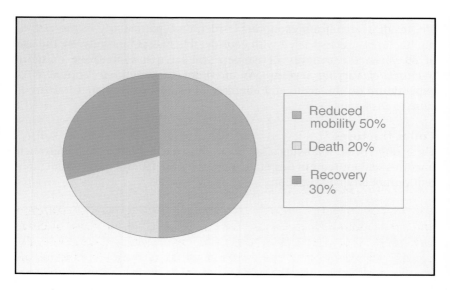

Figure 2.3 Consequences of hip fracture after one year

Vertebral fractures

These are difficult to quantify, as many patients remain asymptomatic until considerable deformity has occurred. Vertebral fractures often present as non-specific back pain and may be undiagnosed for many years. Vertebral fractures lead to a loss of height and curvature of the spine with typical 'dowager's hump' (dorsal kyphosis). Multiple fractures may give rise to loss of height.

RISK FACTORS FOR THE DEVELOPMENT OF OSTEOPOROSIS

These are listed below. In clinical practice the most important factors are early ovarian deficiency and corticosteroid use.

CARDIOVASCULAR DISEASE

The primary endpoints of cardiovascular disease are myocardial infarction and stroke. Although cardiovascular disease is rarely the cause of death in women before the sixth decade, it is the most common cause after the age of 60 years. Most of the evidence for an atherogenic effect of the menopause comes from studies of surgically menopausal women. Oophorectomised women are at two- to three-fold higher risk of coronary heart disease than are age-matched premenopausal women, but some studies find no difference when women who have undergone hysterectomy, but with conservation of ovaries, are used as controls.

CORONARY HEART DISEASE

Coronary heart disease (CHD), is often considered to be a male problem, but there is a growing interest in women. The incidence of coronary heart disease increases after the menopause but the exponential rise with age when age-specific rates are examined is remarkably constant in both sexes. The age-specific death rate is defined as the number of deaths among residents in a defined age group divided by the mid-year average population in that age group. Thus there is no sudden change in the trend for CHD in women at the time of the menopause. The sex ratio does not fall with age, but the absolute difference between female and male age-specific rates not only persists but increases after the menopause. Even in the oldest groups, CHD mortality never 'catches up' with that of men. The 'gender gap' for CHD arises because the exponential rise in mortality rates starts earlier in men. Since in the elderly the female population is larger than the male, the age-specific death rate may provide a more useful figure than simply the total number of deaths.

Table 2.2 Age-specific death rates for men and women from ischaemic heart disease, England and Wales. ONS 2000											
Age (years)	40–44	45–49	50–54	55–59	60–64	65–69	70–74	75–79	80–84	85–89	90+
Rate (male)	0.32	0.65	1.19	2.33	3.85	6.75	11.16	17.46	26.10	35.46	41.99
Rate (female)	0.07	0.14	0.25	0.58	1.21	2.49	5.03	8.88	15.39	24.01	30.00

STROKE

The incidence of stroke increases with age and is a leading cause of death in women. Many survivors are left with significant physical and mental impairment and have serious long-term disability. Stroke can be divided into two main subtypes: ischaemic (the majority) or haemorrhagic. The mechanism of ischaemia (haemodynamic or thromboembolic) and the site of the vascular lesion can classify ischaemic infarction as large vessel atherothrombotic, lacunar, cardioembolic and of undetermined cause. Intracranial haemorrhage can be further divided into subarachnoid haemorrhage or intracerebral haemorrhage, depending on the site and origin of the blood.

RISK FACTORS FOR CARDIOVASCULAR DISEASE AND THE MENOPAUSE

Alterations in lipids, coagulation, insulin sensitivity, endothelial function, inflammatory markers and homocysteine levels and body weight have been described at the menopause.

Lipids

The lipid profile is a well-known predictor of cardiovascular risk. After the menopause the lipid profile changes unfavourably with high-density lipoprotein (HDL) falling and low-density lipoprotein (LDL), lipoprotein(a) and triglycerides rising.

Coagulation

Factor VII, one of the steps of the extrinsic coagulation pathway, which is associated with increased CHD risk rises in postmenopausal women.

Fibrinogen, as well as being the last substrate in the coagulation cascade, is also a marker of inflammatory activity. Fibrinogen is an independent predictor of CVD and menopause is associated with elevated levels. Plasminogen regulation plays an important role in fibrinolysis. Plasminogen activator inhibitor (PAI-1), another predictor of CVD, is also significantly increased after the menopause.

Insulin sensitivity
A reduction in insulin sensitivity has been reported after the menopause. However, most studies have found little or no immediate influence on glucose or insulin metabolism. There is a gradual increase in insulin resistance with menopausal age.

Endothelial function
Endothelial-dependent vasodilatation is reduced in postmenopausal women with normal serum cholesterol and fasting glucose levels.

Inflammatory markers
High levels of leucocyte adhesion molecules and C-reactive protein are associated with an increased risk of CVD, but few studies are available regarding the effect of menopause.

Homocysteine
High levels were first associated as a causal agent in the development of thromboembolic disease. However, recent studies now show an association with CVD, and levels rise after the menopause.

Body weight
Obesity and high blood pressure are independent risk factors for CVD. Whereas menopause is associated with a significant increase in body mass index, blood pressure does not alter after adjusting for age, smoking and body weight.

CONNECTIVE TISSUE ATROPHY

Skin ageing in women is due to a combination of factors, including intrinsic biological ageing, extrinsic damage, particularly ultraviolet radiation and oestrogen deficency. The most obvious signs of ageing are atrophy, laxity, wrinkling, dryness, mottled pigmentation and sparse grey hair; most of these are attributable to chronic ultraviolet exposure rather than intrinsic ageing itself.

Studies in the epidermis indicate that it is thicker in women on taking oestrogen replacement, compared with age-matched untreated women. Cross-sectional studies suggest that the dermis is thickened and has a higher collagen content in postmenopausal HRT users. Some but not all prospective studies show significantly thicker skin with a higher collagen content in women who are given oestrogens. However, a more recent study (Oikarinen 2000) of a one-year treatment with systemic oestrogen alone or combined with progestogen did not show a change in the amount of skin collagen or its rate of synthesis in postmenopausal women.

References

Oikarinen, A. (2000) Systemic estrogens have no conclusive beneficial effect on human skin connective tissue. *Acta Obstet Gynecol Scand* **79**, 250–54.

Stadberg E., Mattsson, L.A. and Milsom, I. (2000) Factors associated with climacteric symptoms and the use of hormone replacement therapy. *Acta Obstet Gynecol Scand* **79**, 286–92.

Office of National Statistics (2000) Mortality Statistics: Cause. Review of the Registrar General on deaths by cause sex and age in England and Wales, 1999 (Series DH2 no. 26).

3 Investigations

Endocrine

These are undertaken to diagnose ovarian failure where appropriate and other causes of vasomotor symptoms, such as abnormalities of thyroid function, phaeochromocytoma, carcinoid syndrome and occasionally mastocytosis.

GONADOTROPHINS AND STEROID HORMONES

Follicle-stimulating hormone (FSH) levels are the only helpful measurement in the diagnosis of ovarian failure. The menopausal range is greater than 30 iu/l. Luteinising hormone (LH), oestradiol, progesterone and testosterone level estimations are of no value. FSH need only be measured if the diagnosis of the menopause is in doubt, and need not be estimated in women of normal menopausal age. However, this needs to be measured in women with suspected premature ovarian failure, i.e. aged less than 40 years. In the perimenopause the daily variation in FSH levels renders this parameter of limited value. FSH levels are of little value in monitoring hormone replacement therapy, since in normal physiology it is controlled by inhibin as well as oestradiol.

THYROID FUNCTION TESTS (FREE T4 AND TSH)

Thyroid disease is more common in women than in men and abnormal thyroid function can lead to symptoms similar to those of the menopause. Thyroid function tests should be done when clinically indicated, particularly if there is inadequate symptomatic response to HRT.

- 24-hour urinary catecholamines: these are used in the diagnosis of phaeochromocytoma.

- 24-hour urinary 5-hydroxyindoleacetic acid: this is used in the diagnosis of carcinoid syndrome.

- 24-hour urine methylhistamine and red cell tryptase: these are measured when mastocytosis is suspected: this is a rare cause of hot flushes. Mastocytosis is a disease characterised by an abnormal increase in mast cells, with the symptoms caused by the release of mast cell mediators.

Endometrial assessment

The principal aim is to exclude premalignant endometrial hyperplasia, i.e. hyperplasia with cytological atypia and carcinoma. A secondary aim is to diagnose structural abnormalities such as endometrial polyps, which can cause irregular bleeding.

BEFORE STARTING HRT

There is no need to assess the endometrium routinely in women with no abnormal bleeding since the incidence of endometrial cancer is less than 0.1%. However, it is essential in those with abnormal bleeding, e.g. a sudden change in menstrual pattern, intermenstrual bleeding, postcoital bleeding or a postmenopausal bleed.

DURING TREATMENT WITH HRT

Endometrial assessment is required when there is abnormal bleeding.

- Cyclical HRT: abnormal bleeding is denoted by a change in pattern of withdrawal bleeds or breakthrough bleeding.

- Continuous combined or long cycle therapy: breakthrough bleeding that persists for more than four to six months or that is not lessening requires assessment. Women who have a bleed after amenorrhoea on a continuous combined regimen need evaluation.

METHODS OF ASSESSMENT

The main methods of assessment are endometrial biopsy, hysteroscopy and transvaginal ultrasound.

Endometrial biopsy
This is essentially a blind procedure and can miss lesions such as polyps, hyperplasia and carcinoma, which develop in localised areas of the uterine cavity. For example, in one study of dilatation and curettage (D&C) abnormalities were missed in six percent of cases. Used alone it is not an adequate method for excluding endometrial malignancy.

Dilatation and curettage does not sample the whole of the endometrium. It is not without risk, e.g. perforation, haemorrhage and even mortality. It is currently being largely replaced by outpatient procedures.

Aspiration curettage is an outpatient procedure that avoids general anaesthesia and has fewer complications than D&C. Various samplers have been developed, such as Vabra, Rockett and Pipelle.

Hysteroscopy

The hysteroscope provides direct visualisation of the endometrial cavity and allows diagnosis of structural abnormalities such as polyps and submucous fibroids. It can now be considered to be the method of choice for the diagnosis of abnormal bleeding. It can be undertaken either under general anaesthesia or as an outpatient procedure with or without local anaesthesia. Even hysteroscopy is not 100% accurate and adenocarcinoma can be missed.

Transvaginal ultrasound

Transvaginal ultrasound measures endometrial thickness. It is also useful in the diagnosis of other pathology, such as fibroids and ovarian lesions. In postmenopausal women an endometrial thickness of less than 4 or 5 mm is suggestive of endometrial atrophy. In a study of over 1000 women with postmenopausal bleeding scheduled for curettage the risk of finding pathological endometrium when the thickness was less than 4 mm was 5.5%. Several studies have been undertaken to examine endometrial thickness in women taking various HRT regimens and it is of concern that there is a wide variation of values and even a 5 mm endometrium may have significant pathological features. While ultrasound is less invasive than endometrial biopsy or hysteroscopy, it does not give a histological diagnosis. A thickened endometrium or a cavity filled with fluid is suggestive of malignancy or other pathology (hyperplasia, polyps).

The instillation of a contrast medium such as saline (sonohysterography) may improve diagnosis of polyps, submucous fibroids and focal thickening of the endometrium. Techniques under assessment are 3-D scanning and Doppler flow and colour imaging.

Assessment of the skeleton

Various methods are available with measurement of bone mineral density using dual-energy X-ray absorptiometry (DXA) currently being considered to be the 'gold standard'.

DUAL-ENERGY X-RAY ABSORPTIOMETRY

DXA uses an X-ray beam with two different energy peaks that are differentially absorbed by bone and soft tissue. The bone mineral content in the area of interest can then be calculated. The dose of ionising radiation is low. Measurements using this technique are conventionally made at the spine and proximal femur but can be made at other sites such as the forearm.

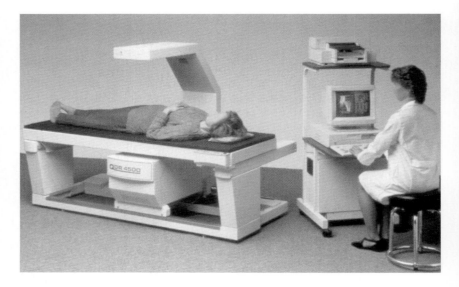

Figure 3.1 A dual energy X-ray machine for measurement of bone mass density

INDICATIONS

It is generally agreed that population screening for osteoporosis is not advised. A DXA scan should only be requested if the result is likely to change management. However, it is important to identify women at increased risk of osteoporosis and therefore fracture. The indications for densitometry are:

- previous fragility fracture
- early surgical or natural menopause (before 45 years)
- premenopausal amenorrhoea of more than six months not due to pregnancy
- hysterectomy with at least one ovary conserved before age 45 years
- predisposing factors such as liver disease, malabsorption, thyroid disease, alcoholism, rheumatoid arthritis
- current or planned long-term oral corticosteroid use (> 5 mg prednisolone or equivalent)
- positive family history of osteoporosis, especially maternal hip fracture.

In addition to the above, women with height loss or kyphosis and X-ray evidence of osteopenia should be considered for a diagnostic DXA scan.

INTERPRETATION OF DXA RESULTS

DXA results are reported as T scores (comparison with young adult mean) and Z scores (comparison with reference values of the same age). The T score relates to absolute fracture risk whereas the Z score relates to the individual's relative risk for their age. (See Table 3.1).

Table 3.1 Quick reference primary care guide on the prevention and treatment of osteoporosis; adapted from Department of Health (1998)		
CATEGORY	FRACTURE RISK	ACTION
NORMAL T score > -1	Low	Lifestyle advice.
OSTEOPENIA T score < -1 to > -2.5	Above average	Lifestyle advice. HRT, especially in women aged 50–60 years. Calcium and vitamin D supplementation.
OSTEOPOROSIS T score < -2.5	High	Lifestyle advice. Treat. Calcium and vitamin D supplementation.
ESTABLISHED OSTEOPOROSIS T score < -2.5 and prevalent fragility fractures	Very high	Lifestyle advice. Pain control. Exclude secondary causes. Treat. Calcium and vitamin D supplementation. Fractures – consider referral.

OTHER

Biochemical markers of bone metabolism

Biochemical markers of bone turnover are classified as markers of resorption or formation. However, it should be remembered that bone resorption and formation are 'coupled' processes and therefore, in most situations, any marker can be used to determine the overall rate of bone turnover.

The principal markers of bone formation are the procollagen peptides of type I collagen, osteocalcin and the bone isoenzyme of alkaline phosphatase.

The most widely used markers of bone resorption are hydroxyproline, hydroxylysine glycosides, pyridinium crosslinks and tartrate resistant acid phosphatase.

A potential use of these markers is to monitor anti-osteoporotic therapy, since they will show changes within three to six months while DXA will take more than one year. However, these markers have not yet been fully evaluated for routine clinical practice.

Quantitative ultrasound (QUS)

This technique involves the transmission of a low amplitude ultrasound beam, usually through the calcaneus, and measures bone strength. It has the attraction of being portable and not using ionising radiation. It remains to be fully evaluated before it can be used in routine clinical practice. In terms of diagnostic capability, the majority of data involves fracture prediction in elderly women, where it appears to be a competent measure of hip fracture risk. However, it remains to be determined whether it can predict fracture at other sites or in younger menopausal women.

Single-energy X-ray absorptiometry

This is a commonly used method for wrist scans.

Quantitative computed tomography (QCT)

This provides measurement of the spine, hip and wrist. It does not have a diagnostic capability superior to that of DXA. Its use in clinical practice is limited by poorer precision and much higher radiation doses than DXA.

Mammography and genetic testing

Breast cancer affects one in ten women in the UK. Rates vary worldwide, with lower rates in some countries such as Japan. A woman's individual risk varies depending on a number of risk factors including family history. Mammography need not be undertaken routinely in women before starting HRT unless the woman is at high risk. There is a wide variation in breast cancer screening programmes throughout the world. In the UK mammography is currently offered three-yearly between the ages of 50 and 65 years.

While it has long been recognised that a proportion of breast cancer cases are the result of an inherited familial predisposition, precise knowledge of the underlying genetic processes has been lacking. Advances in molecular biology, however, have shown that hereditary breast cancer may occur as a result of mutations on several specific gene loci, including *BRCA1*, *BRCA2*, *ATM* gene, PTEN and p53. Several other less frequently occurring predisposition genes such as the androgen receptor gene (AR), the *HNPCC* genes and the oestrogen receptor gene may also be involved, but to a lesser extent. Overall, approximately five to ten percent of all breast cancers are thought to involve one of these inherited predisposition genes, with *BRCA1* and *BRCA2* being responsible for as much as 90% of this group. Because of the complex nature of genetic testing, mutation analysis is not routinely available outside genetic counselling clinics.

The need to provide comprehensive counselling for women with an inherited predisposition to breast cancer has led to the evolution of the familial cancer clinic, involving a multidisciplinary specialist team approach. Familial cancer clinics will provide individuals with information about their risk of developing breast cancer and offer advice regarding further management for high-risk women. The lifetime incidence of breast cancer in mutation carriers is above 50%, and carriers of *BRCA1* mutation also have a substantially increased risk of ovarian cancer. *BRCA1* and *BRCA2* mutations are associated with early-onset breast cancer, and some experts call for aggressive screening of affected persons. Monthly self-examination of the breasts beginning at the age of 18 years and annual clinical examinations and mammography after the age of 25 years have been recommended but are of unproven benefit. Counselling and screening must be undertaken only in specialised centres because of the ethical and legal implications.

4 Benefits of HRT

Short-term benefits

The short-term benefits are relief of vasomotor symptoms, reduction of problems associated with urogenital ageing and relief of psychological symptoms. Patterns of HRT prescribing would suggest that most women take it for symptom control rather than prophylaxis for long-term diseases such as osteoporosis.

VASOMOTOR SYMPTOMS

Hot flushes and night sweats usually improve within four weeks of starting therapy. Relieving night sweats will help to improve sleep patterns and reduce irritability, insomnia and tiredness. Maximum therapeutic response to any particular formulation is usually achieved within three months. Treatment should be continued for at least one year, as otherwise vasomotor symptoms will often recur.

UROGENITAL AGEING

The symptoms resulting from urogenital ageing, such as vaginal dryness and urinary problems, may take as long as a year to respond to oestrogen therapy. Low-dose local oestrogen therapy is often effective and can be used in addition to systemic HRT. Urinary symptoms usually require systemic oestrogen therapy and although irritative symptoms such as urgency, frequency and nocturia may be improved by oestrogens, stress incontinence (due to urethral sphincter incompetence) cannot be treated by oestrogens alone, although it may be improved by a combination of oestrogen and an alpha-adrenergic agonist. Recurrent urinary tract infections may be prevented by oestrogen replacement, but the appropriate dose and duration of therapy have yet to be established.

PSYCHOLOGICAL BENEFITS

Many women report an improvement in psychological wellbeing after starting HRT. There has been much controversy about what this actually means. It has been suggested that oestrogen is a treatment for depressive illness, will restore flagging vigour and confidence and will dispel a host of troublesome psychological difficulties, including sleep disturbance, loss of sexual interest, fatigue, anxiety, oversensitivity, tearfulness, guilt and aggression. However, it must be remembered that there is a large placebo effect. Relief of vasomotor symptoms, especially night sweats, may also contribute. Furthermore, relief of vaginal dryness and dyspareunia are important factors.

Long-term benefits

The major long-term benefit of HRT is the prevention of osteoporosis. It also seems to reduce the risk of cardiovascular disease, but this issue is fraught with controversy. The risk of Alzheimer's disease may be reduced, as may that of bowel cancer. Other benefits include a reduction of tooth loss, adult macular degeneration, falls and osteoarthritis and improved wound healing.

OSTEOPOROSIS

The efficacy of HRT in the prevention and treatment of osteoporosis is well established. Some bone gain may be anticipated in the initial 18 to 24 months, but thereafter bone mineral density values tend to plateau. The bone protection of HRT lasts as long as the regimen is taken and stops on cessation of treatment. It was initially assumed that five to ten years of HRT use after the menopause would delay peak hip fracture incidence by a corresponding amount. Thus if the median age of hip fracture is 79 years, and if this is delayed by five to ten years, then most women would not live long enough to suffer a hip fracture. However, it is now evident that five to ten years of HRT soon after the menopause does not confer sufficient skeletal protection to give any significant risk reduction of hip fracture three decades later. Therefore, for effective prevention of hip fracture, HRT needs to be taken lifelong and continuously.

The 'standard' bone-protective doses of oestrogen were said to be oestradiol 2 mg, conjugated equine oestrogens 0.625 mg and transdermal 50 μg patch. However, it is now evident that lower doses are protective. Surprisingly, only two randomised trials of HRT with the endpoint being fracture rather than bone density have been undertaken. Both show a reduction in fractures. There is evidence that the higher oestrogen levels obtained with subcutaneous oestrogen implants cause a truly anabolic bone gain as opposed to an anti-catabolic prevention of loss. With regard to progestogens, there is some evidence that 19-nortestosterone derivatives may enhance oestrogenic bone gain. Tibolone is also bone-protective. Women with a pre-existing vertebral fracture are a particularly good group to target for any anti-fracture treatment as they have a 1.5- to four-fold increased risk of appendicular fractures compared with women without vertebral fractures.

Some women have no bone response to HRT, despite good compliance with therapy. A recent prospective study (Komulainen *et al.* 2000) shows that current smokers and women with low body weight are at increased risk of poor bone response to HRT.

CARDIOVASCULAR DISEASE

Until 1998 it was accepted that HRT reduced the incidence of cardiovascular disease. Observational epidemiological studies strongly suggested a protective effect. The protective effect was supported by experimental *in vitro*, and *in vivo* animal and human studies of arterial function and biochemical markers such as plasma lipoproteins. The beneficial effects of HRT on the cardiovascular system may be mediated by several mechanisms, including alterations in lipids, coagulation, insulin sensitivity and endothelial function. Opinions have varied on the strength of the evidence that HRT reduces the risk of CHD, since observational studies could have significant bias related to the inclusion of healthy women who were HRT users.

Primary and secondary prevention randomised placebo-controlled trials are necessary to quantify benefits and risks reliably. The aim of a primary prevention trial is to determine if women without the disease of interest can be prevented from developing it. In contrast, secondary prevention trials examine if various interventions can prevent disease recurrence. It is important to distinguish between primary and secondary prevention, since it is likely that an endothelium with an established atherosclerotic plaque will respond differently from one that has not.

PRIMARY PREVENTION OF CORONARY HEART DISEASE

In a meta-analysis of 16 prospective observational studies, 15 showed a benefit for CHD. The Framingham study was the only prospective study to report an increase in CHD risk in women using HRT.

Cohort studies with internal controls showed a combined reduction in CHD risk of 42% in HRT users. There is some concern that any cardioprotective effect of oestrogen could be attenuated by addition of a progestogen, since the benefits of HRT have mostly been seen in women who took unopposed equine oestrogens. No difference has been found between oestrogen alone and oestrogen combined with progestogen. A report from the Nurses' Health Study has shown that women using oestrogen-only HRT had an adjusted relative risk for major coronary heart disease of 0.60 (0.43–0.83), while women using combined preparations had an adjusted risk of 0.39 (0.19–0.78). A Swedish study of routine prescription and hospitalisation records reported a relative risk for myocardial infarction of 0.53 (0.30–0.87) in women using a combined oestrogen and progestogen preparation.

Two randomised placebo-controlled primary prevention trials are in progress. The Women's Health Initiative (WHI), which started in 1993 and will run to 2007, tests the effect of HRT and that of calcium and vitamin D supplementation and dietary modification, using a factorial design. In the HRT arms of the trial, the WHI has enrolled 27 300 women aged 50–79 years from 45 centres in the USA. The other similar study is the Women's International Study of Long Duration Oestrogen after the Menopause (WISDOM), which will randomise 34 000 women aged 50–64 years, about half of whom will be from the UK. This started in 1998, and will treat women for ten years and follow them for a further ten years. Both WHI and WISDOM will compare combined HRT with oestrogen-only HRT in women who have had a hysterectomy.

SECONDARY PREVENTION OF CORONARY HEART DISEASE

The most positive results of secondary prevention with HRT come from angiographic studies. These showed marked survival benefits that were greatest in women with the most severe coronary stenosis. Analysis of the Nurses' Health Study reported a relative risk for mortality in current HRT users with at least one major CHD risk factor of 0.51 (0.45–0.57) compared with only 0.89 (0.62–1.28) for current users with no risk factors (Grodstein et al. 1997).

For women who have survived a first myocardial infarction, a cohort study of 981 cases showed no difference in the risk of recurrent coronary events between current users of hormone therapy and other women (adjusted relative hazard [RH]: 0.96; 95% CI: 0.62–1.50) (Heckbert et al. 2001). Relative to the risk in women not currently using hormones, there was a suggestion of increased risk during the first 60 days after starting hormone therapy (RH: 2.16; 95% CI: 0.94–4.95) and reduced risk with current hormone use for longer than one year (RH: 0.76; 95% CI: 0.42–1.36). These results are consistent with the findings of the randomised controlled trial (HERS) reported below. The Nurses' Health Study has also shown an increased risk in recurrent major coronary events among short-term hormone users with previous coronary disease but to decrease with longer-term use (Grodstein et al. 2001).

A number of randomised trials have been set up. These trials may be confounded by the fact that the women involved may have other coronary risk factors (diabetes, smoking, obesity) and multiple drugs may be taken as a secondary intervention (statins, antihypertensives, aspirin). The Heart and Estrogen/Progestin Replacement Study (HERS), which enrolled 2763 women with established CHD with an average follow-up of four years, reported its essentially negative findings at least in the first year of treatment. The treatment group was given continuous combined conjugated equine oestrogens and medroxyprogesterone acetate. There were no differences between non-fatal myocardial infarction, CHD death, unstable angina or coronary revascularisation in the two groups. There were significant trends for a reduction with time in primary CHD events and non-fatal myocardial infarction. However, on a year-to-year basis there was no statistically significant difference between the HRT and the placebo groups.

The Estrogen Replacement and Atherosclerosis (ERA) trial was a three-arm, randomised, placebo-controlled, double-blind trial to evaluate the effects of oestrogen replacement therapy (0.625 mg/day oral conjugated oestrogen) with or without continuous progestogen (2.5 mg oral medroxyprogesterone acetate/day) versus placebo on progression of atherosclerosis in 309 women over three years. The primary outcome of interest was the change in minimum diameter of the major epicardial segments, as assessed by quantitative coronary angiography. The study showed that neither oestrogen alone nor oestrogen plus medroxyprogesterone affected the progression of coronary atherosclerosis in women with established disease.

At least four other secondary prevention trials are under way using angiographically defined endpoints (known by their acronyms WELLHART, EAGAR, WHISP and WAVE). These trials are recruiting relatively few patients (200–400) and have shorter periods of observation (three years) compared with trials (such as HERS) that use CHD events and mortality as primary endpoints.

STROKE

The data for stroke are unclear, and randomised trials are limited. A substantial body of observational data exists on the use of HRT. However, interpretation is complicated by the differences in study design, failure to differentiate between ischaemic and haemorrhagic stroke and status of HRT use (current versus ever-users). An analysis of the Nurses' Health Study showed no increase in stroke, except when high-dose oestrogen was used (Grodstein *et al.* 2000). Furthermore, the HERS investigators showed no increase in stroke in this randomised controlled trial.

ALZHEIMER'S DISEASE

Alzheimer's disease accounts for about 70% of the people who have one of the disorders categorised as dementia. It is becoming a major worldwide problem with increasing longevity of the population. The number of people suffering from Alzheimer's disease rises exponentially with increasing age. In women, the role of oestrogen deficiency is suggested by the observations that Alzheimer's disease is more common in thin women (less peripheral conversion in fat of steroid precursors to oestrogen), and in those who have suffered either a previous myocardial infarction or hip fracture. The mechanisms of action of oestrogen on brain function are unclear. Studies have shown that oestrogen stimulates neuronal function, increases the number of developed gliacytes, increases cerebral blood flow, suppresses amyloid deposition, improves cholinergic transmission and protects from the oxidative stress induced by amyloid deposition.

Several epidemiological studies have suggested that oestrogen use may delay or prevent the onset of Alzheimer's disease with the risk decreasing with both increasing dose and duration of use. Furthermore, the age of onset of Alzheimer's disease was later in women who had taken oestrogen. However, HRT does not slow disease progression or improve global, cognitive or functional outcomes in women with established mild to moderate Alzheimer's disease.

Other benefits

There is now evidence that women taking HRT have a lower risk of colon cancer, but the mechanisms involved have not been elucidated. Meta-analysis has shown a 20% reduction in the risk of colon cancer among current users. It may also be involved in wound healing. It can also improve balance and reduce tooth loss. A reduction in falls has the potential to have a significant effect on fracture. Age-related macular degeneration and cataract are leading causes of blindness and several studies now show a reduction in the incidence of these conditions in HRT users. Cataract and dry eye are also improved. Furthermore, long-term HRT use has been reported as having a non-significant protective effect against the development of hip osteoarthritis in elderly white women (Dennison *et al.* 1998).

References

Dennison, E.M., Arden, N.K. and Kellingray, S. *et al.* (1998) Hormone replacement therapy, other reproductive variables and symptomatic hip osteoarthritis in elderly white women: a case-control study. *Br J Rheumatol* **37**, 1198–202.

Grodstein, F., Stampfer, M.J. and Colditz, G.A. *et al.* (1997) Postmenopausal hormone therapy and mortality. *N Engl J Med* **336**, 1769–75.

Grodstein F. Manson J.E. Colditz G.A. *et al.* (2000) A prospective, observational study of postmenopausal hormone therapy and primary prevention of cardiovascular disease. *Ann Intern Med* **133**, 933–41.

Grodstein, F., Manson, J.E. and Stampfer, M.J. (2001) Postmenopausal hormone use and secondary prevention of coronary events in the nurses' health study: a prospective, observational study. *Ann Intern Med* **135**, 1–8.

Heckbert, S.R., Kaplan, R.C., Weiss, N.S. *et al.* (2001) Risk of recurrent coronary events in relation to use and recent initiation of postmenopausal hormone therapy. *Arch Intern Med* **161**, 1709–13.

Komulainen, M., Kroger, H., Tuppurainen, M.T. *et al.* (2000) Identification of early postmenopausal women with no bone response to HRT: results of a five-year clinical trial. *Osteoporos Int* **11**, 211–8.

5 Risks of HRT

The risks of HRT are one of the major reasons for stopping therapy. These need to be balanced against the suggestion that long-term HRT prevents disease and prolongs life. The three main areas of concern are breast and endometrial cancer and venous thromboembolic disease. Other conditions will be dealt with in Chapter 7.

Breast cancer

Breast cancer is the reason most commonly given by women for not wanting to take long-term HRT, with a 50-year-old having about a ten percent chance of developing it during her remaining lifetime. The incidence of breast cancer varies between different populations. In North America and Europe the cumulative incidence of breast cancer between the ages of 50 and 70 years in never-users of HRT is about 45 per 1000 women. A re-analysis undertaken in 1997 of 51 epidemiological studies including 52 705 women with and 108 411 without breast cancer found that HRT increases the risk by 2.3% per year of use, when it is started in the 50+ years age group. This magnitude of increase is roughly equivalent to the rise in relative risk of breast cancer associated with each year the menopause is delayed after the age of 50 years. Such an effect is not seen in women who start HRT early for a premature menopause, indicating that it is the duration of lifetime oestrogen exposure that is relevant. After cessation of HRT use, the effect on breast cancer falls and has disappeared within five years (Table 5.1).

Breast cancers occurring in women taking HRT appear to have a better prognosis than non-users, with a 16% reduction in mortality. While this

Table 5.1 Breast cancer and HRT (data derived from Collaborative Group on Hormonal Factors in Breast Cancer 1997)

Years of HRT use	Extra cases per 1000 HRT users
5	2
10	6
15	12

may be due to increased surveillance, it can also be due to differences in the biology of these tumours. The tumours are more localised and less aggressive than in never-users. There is little evidence that use of HRT in patients with a family history of breast cancer will further increase their risk. Similarly, there is no convincing evidence that breast cancer risk is increased in patients with benign disease.

Combined oestrogen/progestin versus oestrogen-only HRT has become an extremely topical subject. Studies so far have not been randomised and data have been presented in slightly different ways. It would appear that breast cancer risk is greater in combined HRT users, and this may be more pronounced in lean women. The studies refute the notion that progestogens protect against breast cancer development, and any recommendation of their use in hysterectomised women for this indication. The issue of different progestogens and regimens is unclear: a greater risk has been found with cyclic than with continuous administration of 17-hydroxyprogesterone derivatives, but the converse has been found with 19-nortestosterone derivatives. The increased risk of breast cancer with progestogen addition has to be balanced against the reduction in risk of endometrial cancer provided by combined therapy.

It must also be remembered that the increased risk of breast cancer found in nulliparous women, those who delay their first birth or who have a family history of breast cancer may be higher than that conferred by HRT.

Breast cancer survivors who request HRT pose a management problem, since there is no evidence from randomised controlled trials. Standard advice is to stop medication at the time of diagnosis and avoid future use of exogenous oestrogens. The various clinical studies of breast cancer patients who have been prescribed HRT have not shown an adverse effect on survival. However, these involved small numbers with short-term follow-up. Low-dose vaginal oestrogens, such as oestradiol and oestriol, are not absorbed systemically to any significant degree and are not contraindicated in women with a previous breast cancer. In women where the sole endpoint of treatment is the prevention or treatment of osteoporosis, bisphosphonates are a good option. An issue that needs addressing is that of women who have survived breast cancer in their 30s and have undergone premature ovarian failure as a consequence of chemotherapy.

Endometrial cancer

The link between unopposed postmenopausal oestrogen replacement therapy and endometrial cancer was first reported in the 1970s. The effect of unopposed oestrogen therapy increasing the risk of developing endometrial hyperplasia and carcinoma has been reviewed in a meta-analysis of 30 studies. The summary relative risk (RR) was 2.3 for oestrogen users compared with non-users with a 95% CI of 2.1–2.5. The risk of endometrial cancer death is also raised. The relative risk increased with prolonged duration of use (RR 9.5 for ten or more years). The risk of endometrial cancer remained elevated for five or more years after discontinuation of unopposed oestrogen therapy (RR 2.3). Interrupting oestrogen for five to seven days per month does not reduce risk. Recent case–control studies (Weiderpass *et al.* 1999a, 1999b) have shown similar findings. Relative risk increases by 17% per year of use. Randomised controlled trials have shown an increased risk of endometrial hyperplasia with unopposed oestrogen being 20% at one year and 62% at three years. It is controversial whether different types of oestrogen differ in risk, with studies producing conflicting findings. With regard to low-potency oestrogen, oral but not vaginal oestriol increases the risk of endometrial cancer and atypical hyperplasia.

Progestogen addition has been advocated for many years with the intention of preventing hyperplasia and carcinoma. Meta-analysis shows that the overall summary RR for endometrial cancer was 0.8 (CI 0.6–1.2). In contrast with unopposed oestrogen, no substantial elevation of relative risk remains five years or more after stopping therapy. Ten days or more of progestogen are recommended for monthly sequential regimens, but there has been some debate about this. No increased risk of endometrial cancer has been found with continuous combined regimens. There is debate about the relative merits of different progestogens; however, studies have not examined equivalent doses. The increased risk of endometrial cancer in HRT users has to be compared with that found in obese and diabetic women, where it is higher.

Management in women with a previous endometrial cancer depends on the extent of myometrial invasion, histology and whether or not there is cervical and uterine involvement. Patients with stage I endometrial cancer can be considered for oestrogen therapy. There is some debate about whether opposed or unopposed HRT should be used. Progestogens alone can be used to counteract vasomotor symptoms.

Venous thromboembolic disease

Exogenous oestrogens used in the combined oral contraceptive pill have long been recognised as causative factors in the pathogenesis of venous thromboembolism (VTE). Until 1996 HRT was not thought to increase the risk of venous thromboembolism. A recent series of case–control studies (Daly *et al.* 1996, Grodstein *et al.* 1996, Jick *et al.* 1996, Guttham *et al.* 1996) and one randomised controlled trial (Hulley *et al.* 1998) provide clear evidence linking this treatment and VTE; with a relative risk of between two and four and an absolute risk of around three per 10 000 users per year.

One study suggested that the increased risk was restricted to the first year of use. The baseline risk of VTE in menopausal women is low being of the order of one in 10 000 per year. This means that for 10 000 women-years of use, HRT would be responsible for two extra cases of VTE that would otherwise not have occurred. The mortality rate of VTE is 1–2%.

The mechanisms as to why HRT provokes an increased risk of VTE are unclear. The study suggesting that the increased risk is restricted to the first year of use raises the possibility that HRT interacts with and unmasks previously undiagnosed thrombophilic abnormalities.

The haemostatic system is altered with HRT, but does not appear to be the sole mechanism by which the risk of VTE is increased. Markers for VTE are the coagulation inhibitors antithrombin III, protein C and protein S. A decrease is associated with a higher risk of VTE. The effects of HRT and oestrogen replacement are controversial. Antithrombin III and protein S levels fall, with oestrogen replacement showing a higher reduction than HRT. Protein C is increased with oestrogen alone, but decreased with HRT. It would seem that the overall effect of these and other changes tilts the balance in favour of VTE.

The evidence base relating VTE risk factors and HRT is scanty, and advice and management strategies have to depend on clinical 'logic' and opinion. The absolute risk of VTE and HRT is low and in general the benefits with respect to prevention of osteoporosis and control of menopausal symptoms that may severely affect quality of life are likely to outweigh the small risk of VTE. Women commencing HRT should be evaluated for VTE risk factors on an individual basis and advised not only of the potential benefits but also of the small risk of venous thrombosis. When taking the history it is important to assess the family history, the severity of personal events and whether or not any were objectively confirmed. A personal history of VTE is the single biggest risk for a future episode. After a single episode of VTE when anticoagulation is discontinued there is a constant recurrence risk of five percent per annum.

Screening for thrombophilic defects should be restricted to selected women: those with a personal or family history of VTE. However, it is vital that a negative screen for known causes of thrombophilia is not used as false reassurance in women with a personal history of VTE, since they are still at considerable risk of recurrence. Women aged 50 years or over with a history of VTE within the previous year, in addition to thrombophilia screening, should be screened for underlying disease, including malignancy and connective tissue disorders.

Data regarding the combination of HRT use and thrombophilias are limited. It would appear that HRT increases the relative risk of VTE substantially, especially if the thrombophilic defects are multiple. Women with severe thrombophilic defects, such as antithrombin deficiency, combinations of defects or acquired antiphospholipid syndromes, may be advised to avoid HRT unless it is used in conjunction with prophylactic anticoagulation. Women with a family history of VTE with no laboratory evidence of thrombophilia, providing they are counselled about VTE risk, in general may consider using HRT. The evidence as to whether the transdermal route is superior to the oral one is poor, although many experts tend to favour the former. Until recently it was thought that progestogens in high dose did not increase the risk of VTE and were a useful option for vasomotor symptom control in women at increased risk of VTE. However, recent studies (Vasilakis *et al.* 1999) show that progestogens in non-contraceptive doses also increase the risk of VTE. As with breast cancer survivors, bisphosphonates are a useful option in women whose sole endpoint of treatment is the prevention and treatment of osteoporosis (note that raloxifene also increases the risk of VTE).

HRT should be added as a risk factor for VTE when assessing patients preoperatively, but there is no evidence at present to support a policy of routinely stopping HRT prior to surgery, providing appropriate thromboprophylaxis is used.

References

Collaborative Group on Hormonal Factors in Breast Cancer (1997). Breast Cancer and HRT: collaborative reanalysis of data from 51 epidemiological studies of 52,705 women with breast cancer and 108,411 women without breast cancer. *Lancet* **350**, 1047–59.

Daly, E., Vessey, M.P., Hawkins, M.M. *et al.* (1996) Risk of venous thromboembolism in users of hormone replacement therapy. *Lancet*, **348**, 977–80.

Grodstein, F., Stampfer, M.J., Goldhaber, S.Z. *et al.* (1996) Prospective study of exogenous hormones and risk of pulmonary embolism in women. *Lancet* **348**, 983–7.

Guttham, S.P., Rodriguez, L.A.G., Castellsague, J. and Oliart, A.D. (1997) Hormone replacement therapy and risk of venous thromboembolism: population based case-control study. *Br Med J* **314**, 796–800.

Hulley, S., Grady, D., Bush, T. *et al.* (1998) Randomized trial of estrogen plus progestin for secondary prevention of coronary heart disease in postmenopausal women. Heart and Estrogen/progestin Replacement Study (HERS) Research Group. *JAMA* **280**, 605–13.

Jick, H., Derby, L.E., Myers, M.W., Vasilakis, C. and Newton, K.M. (1996) Risk of hospital admission for idiopathic venous thromboembolism among users of postmenopausal oestrogens. *Lancet* **348**, 981–3.

Vasilakis C., Jick, H., del Mar Melero-Montes, M. (1999) Risk of idiopathic venous thromboembolism in users of progestagens alone. *Lancet* **354**, 1610–1.

Weiderpass, E., Adami, H.O., Baron, J.A. *et al.* (1999a) Risk of endometrial cancer following estrogen replacement with and without progestins. *J Natl Cancer Inst* **9**, 1131–7.

Weiderpass, E., Baron, J.A., Adami, H.O. *et al.* (1999b) Low-potency oestrogen and risk of endometrial cancer: a case-control study. *Lancet* **353**, 1824–8.

6 HRT: preparations, prescribing, treatment duration and management of adverse effects

Over the past few years there has been a dramatic increase in the number of licensed HRT preparations available. The essential component is oestrogen, which is combined with a progestogen to prevent endometrial hyperplasia in women whose uterus is intact. HRT can be delivered by a variety of routes: oral, transdermal, subcutaneous, vaginal and intranasal.

Steroids used in HRT

OESTROGENS

Oestrogen are classified into two types: natural and synthetic. Natural oestrogens include oestradiol, oestrone and oestriol, of which most are chemically synthesised from soya beans or yams. Conjugated equine oestrogens, also classed as natural, contain about 50–65% oestrone sulphate and the remainder consists of equine oestrogens, mainly equilin sulphate. Synthetic oestrogens, such as ethinyl oestradiol and mestranol,

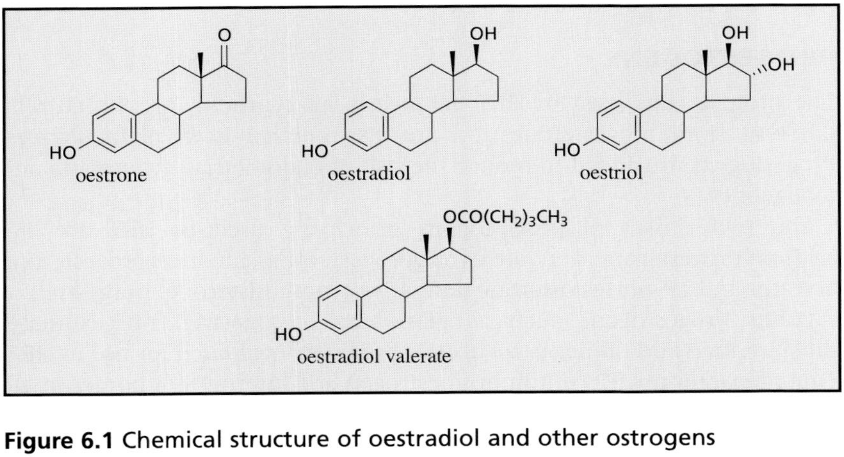

Figure 6.1 Chemical structure of oestradiol and other ostrogens

are less suitable for HRT because of their greater metabolic impact.

Until recently, the generally accepted minimum bone sparing doses of oestrogen were oral oestradiol 2 mg, conjugated equine oestrogens 0.625 mg and transdermal oestradiol 50 µg patch. However, there is increasing evidence that lower doses are effective, for example oral oestradiol 1 mg, esterified oestrogens 0.3 mg and 25 µg transdermally. Similarly, low doses of oestrogen are useful in treating hot flushes. Oral oestradiol 1 mg is as effective as 2 mg in reducing hot flushes.

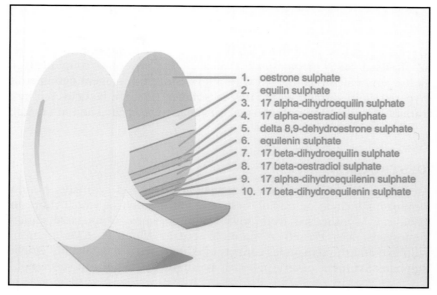

1. oestrone sulphate
2. equilin sulphate
3. 17 alpha-dihydroequilin sulphate
4. 17 alpha-oestradiol sulphate
5. delta 8,9-dehydroestrone sulphate
6. equilenin sulphate
7. 17 beta-dihydroequilin sulphate
8. 17 beta-oestradiol sulphate
9. 17 alpha-dihydroequilenin sulphate
10. 17 beta-dihydroequilenin sulphate

Figure 6.2 Conjugated equine oestrogens

PROGESTOGENS

The progestogens used in HRT are nearly all synthetic, are structurally different from progesterone and are also derived from plant sources. Progestogens are added to reduce the risk of endometrial hyperplasia and malignancy.

The two classes of progestogens principally used in HRT are 17-hydroxyprogesterone derivatives (dydrogesterone, medroxyprogesterone acetate) and 19-nortestosterone derivatives (norethisterone, norgestrel).

Other progestogens such as gestodene, desogestrel, norgestimate, drospirenone and nomegestrol acetate are being evaluated for use in HRT. One preparation with continuous oestrogen and intermittent norgestimate administration is available.

Currently progestogens are mainly given orally, although norethisterone

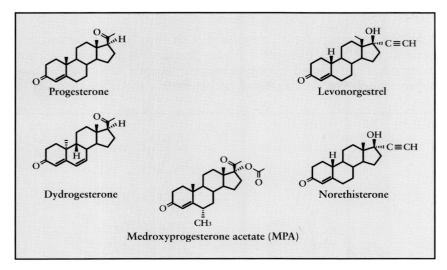

Figure 6.3 Chemical structure of some progestogens

and levonorgestrel are available in transdermal patches combined with oestradiol, and levonorgestrel can be delivered directly to the uterus. Progesterone itself is formulated as a 4% vaginal gel and is licensed for use in HRT. A progesterone pessary to be used vaginally or rectally is available but currently is not licensed for HRT in the UK. See Table 6.1.

Table 6.1   Daily doses of progestogen in various HRT preparations

Drug	Dose	Regimen
Monthly sequential		
Norethisterone oral	1 mg	Last 10–14 days of a 28-day cycle
Norethisterone patch	170 µg or 250 µg	Last 14 days of a 28-day cycle
Levonorgestrel oral	75–250 µg	Last 10–12 days of a 28-day cycle
Levonorgestrel patch	20 µg	Last 14 days of a 28-day cycle
Medroxyprogesterone acetate	10 mg	Last 14 days of a 28-day cycle
Dydrogesterone	10–20 mg	Last 14 days of a 28-day cycle
Long cycle		
Medroxyprogesterone acetate	20 mg	Last 14 days of a 3-month cycle
Continuous combined		
Norethisterone	0.5–1 mg	
Medroxyprogesterone acetate	2.5–5.0 mg	

TIBOLONE

Tibolone is a synthetic compound that has mixed oestrogenic, progestogenic and androgenic actions because of its three different metabolites and is used in postmenopausal women who wish to have amenorrhoea. The Δ4 metabolite, as opposed to the other two, has no

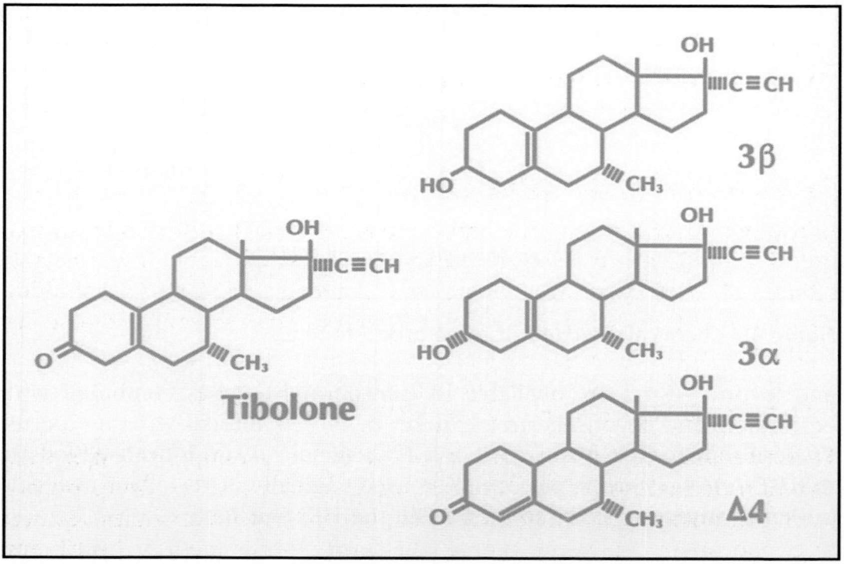

Figure 6.4 Chemical structure of tibolone and its metabolites

oestrogenic activity and binds only to androgen and progesterone receptors. This metabolite is produced in the endometrium and accounts for the amenorrhoea found in the majority (80%) of women. It is used to treat vasomotor, psychological and libido problems. It can be used for osteoporosis prevention and the bone-sparing dose is 2.5 mg daily.

ANDROGENS

Testosterone implants may be used to improve libido, but are not successful in all women since other factors such as marital problems, depression, concomitant drug therapy (e.g. SSRIs, beta-blockers) may be involved.

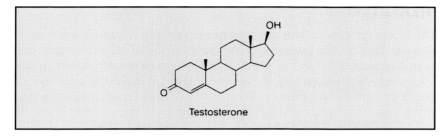

OH

O

Testosterone

Figure 6.5 Chemical structure of testosterone

Delivery systems

ORAL ADMINISTRATION

In routine clinical practice the oral route is the usual first line of treatment unless there is a pre-existing medical condition. All currently available tablets of oestrogen and progestogen except Femulen® (etynodiol diacetate) contain lactose as a bulking agent and are not suitable for women with lactose sensitivity.

PARENTERAL ADMINISTRATION

Transdermal Oestradiol and progestogens can penetrate through skin. Two transdermal systems are now available – patch and gel. There are two patch technologies; alcohol-based reservoir patches with an adhesive outer ring and matrix patches where the hormone is evenly distributed throughout the adhesive. Skin reactions are less common with matrix than reservoir patches. Only norethisterone and levonorgestrel are delivered transdermally in patches. At present only oestradiol is delivered in a gel.

Implants Oestradiol implants are crystalline pellets of oestradiol that are inserted subcutaneously under local anaesthetic, releasing oestradiol over many months. Implants have the advantage that once inserted the patient does not have to remember to take medication. A significant concern is tachyphylaxis, defined as recurrence of menopausal symptoms while the implant is still releasing adequate levels of oestradiol. A check on plasma oestradiol should be considered prior to re-implantation to ensure that the level is in the normal range (< 1000 pmol/l). There are also concerns that implants may remain effective for many years. This needs to be remembered for non-hysterectomised women.

Other Oestradiol and progestogens can also be absorbed from the vagina and nasal mucosa, leading to the development of vaginal rings and nasal sprays that are now available.

INTRAUTERINE

The levonorgestrel intrauterine system delivers intrauterine progestogen, and can provide the progestogen component of HRT. The oestrogen can then be given orally or transdermally. It also provides a solution to the problem of contraception in the perimenopause. It is also the only way in which a 'no bleed' regimen can be achieved in perimenopausal women.

ORAL VERSUS PARENTERAL ADMINISTRATION

The advantages of oral versus transdermal therapy are highly debated, mainly for oestrogen. The transdermal route avoids the gut and first-pass effect on the liver. After oral administration the dominant circulating oestrogen is oestrone, but after parenteral administration it is oestradiol. However, all oestrogens, regardless of the route of administration, eventually pass through the liver and are recycled by the enterohepatic circulation.

Substances produced by the liver may be differentially affected by the two routes. For example, high doses of conjugated equine oestrogens increase the production of renin substrate, but the type induced is not the one normally associated with hypertension. The clinical significance is unclear, since blood pressure does not increase on this form of HRT. Also, production of certain coagulation factors and lipids may be differentially affected by the route of administration.

For example, oral oestrogens lower plasma levels of low density lipoproteins (LDL) and lipoprotein (a) (Lp(a)), protect these lipoproteins from oxidation and increase levels of high density lipoproteins (HDL). These changes would be considered desirable, but may be accompanied by an increase in fasting triglyceride levels. Non-oral oestrogens have less effect on plasma levels of LDL and Lp(a), but protect them from oxidation, and either have no effect on or in some cases reduce levels of HDL and fasting triglyceride.

Thus currently there appears to be no clear advantage to the transdermal over the oral route.

Prescribing HRT

HYSTERECTOMISED WOMEN

It has been estimated that, by the age of 55 years, 20% of women in the UK will have undergone hysterectomy, but the rates vary between different countries. In general hysterectomised women need to be given oestrogen alone and there is no requirement for a progestogen. Recent studies (Ross *et al*. 2000, Schairer *et al*. 2000) showing an increase in breast cancer risk in women prescribed oestrogen plus progestogen compared with oestrogen alone do not justify the addition of progestogen for these women.

NON-HYSTERECTOMISED WOMEN

These women require combined therapy of progestogen and oestrogen to reduce the increased risk of endometrial hyperplasia and carcinoma that occurs with oestrogen alone. Progestogen must be given to women who have undergone endometrial ablative techniques since it cannot be assumed that all the endometrium has been removed, even if they have been amenorrhoeic.

Progestogen can either be given for 10–14 days every four weeks, for 14 days every 13 weeks or every day continuously. The first leads to monthly bleeds, the second to three-monthly bleeds and the last aims to achieve amenorrhoea.

PERIMENOPAUSAL WOMEN

There is no need to wait for 12 months of amenorrhoea before starting HRT. Symptoms of ovarian failure such hot flushes, mood changes and vaginal dryness commonly start in the menopause transition and are often accompanied by erratic menstruation. Continuous combined regimens should not be used in perimenopausal women because of the risk of irregular bleeding, since they have spontaneous ovarian activity.

The options available are monthly cyclic or three-monthly cyclic regimens. For women with infrequent menstruation or who are intolerant of progestogen a three-monthly preparation should be considered.

POSTMENOPAUSAL WOMEN

The regular withdrawal bleeds induced by sequential therapy are considered to be unacceptable by many postmenopausal women who will prefer 'no bleed' therapy. This is not surprising since women in western societies will experience about 400 menstruations between the menarche and the menopause. Adherence to therapy is higher in those prescribed continuous combined than monthly therapy because of a dislike of a return of monthly bleeds.

Women are considered to be postmenopausal 12 months after their last menstrual period. However, in clinical practice the definition is difficult to apply for women who started HRT in the perimenopause and wish to switch to 'no bleed' therapy. Pragmatically, postmenopausal status can be estimated from:

- **Age** It has been estimated that by the age of 54 years, 80% of women are postmenopausal.

- **Previous amenorrhoea or elevated follicle-stimulating hormone (FSH)** It is likely that a women who has experienced six months' amenorrhoea or had an elevated FSH in her mid-40s will be postmenopausal after taking several years of monthly sequential HRT.

'No bleed' therapy can be achieved with continuous combined oestrogen and progestogen or tibolone, which induce endometrial atrophy. Irregular bleeding or spotting can occur during the first four to six months of treatment and does not warrant investigation. Endometrial assessment needs to be considered if the bleeding is getting heavier rather than lighter, if it persists beyond six months, or if it occurs after a significant time of amenorrhoea. However, there are some women who have persistent irregular bleeding with a normal uterus and may wish to return to sequential therapy.

Treatment of urogenital symptoms

Some women only wish to have treatment of urogenital symptoms, and not take systemic HRT. Synthetic oestrogens should be avoided since they are well absorbed from the vagina. The options available are low-dose natural oestrogens such as vaginal oestriol (cream or pessary) or oestradiol (tablet or ring). Long-term treatment is required, since symptoms return on cessation of therapy. With the recommended dose regimens, no adverse endometrial effects should be incurred and progestogen need not be added for endometrial protection with such low-dose preparations.

Urogenital symptoms can occur even with systemic HRT in doses sufficient to deal with hot flushes. In these women vaginal oestrogens need to be added. Some women may wish to use vaginal lubricants or long-acting bioadhesive moisturisers instead of oestrogen.

Duration of treatment

This needs to be discussed with each individual woman, and depends on the endpoints of treatment.

TREATMENT OF VASOMOTOR SYMPTOMS

Treatment should be continued for up to five years and then stopped to evaluate whether symptoms have recurred. This duration will not significantly increase the risk of breast cancer.

PREVENTION OR TREATMENT OF OSTEOPOROSIS

For this issue treatment needs to be continued lifelong, as bone mineral density falls when treatment is stopped. It has been assumed that five to ten years of HRT use after the menopause would delay the peak hip fracture incidence by a corresponding amount. Thus, if the median age of hip fracture is 79 years, and if this is delayed by five to ten years through using HRT, then most women would not live long enough to suffer a hip fracture. However, recent epidemiological evidence suggests that five to ten years of HRT soon after the menopause does not give any significant risk reduction of hip fracture 30 years later. While some women will be happy to take HRT lifelong, others may view treatment as a continuum of options and wish to change to other agents, such as bisphosphonates, because of the breast cancer risk with long-term use.

PREMATURE MENOPAUSE

Here women are usually advised to continue with HRT until the average age of the natural menopause, i.e. 51 years. Thereafter the issues discussed in the above sections pertain.

Managing the adverse effects of hormone replacement therapy

Adverse effects account for almost 35% of HRT discontinuations and can be either oestrogen- or progestogen-related, or a combination of both. Problems with bleeding and a fear of weight gain are also common complaints.

OESTROGENIC-RELATED ADVERSE EFFECTS

These include fluid retention, bloating, breast tenderness or enlargement, nausea, headaches, leg cramps and dyspepsia. They occur continuously or randomly throughout the cycle. In most cases they are transient and resolve with continued use. Patients should be encouraged to persist with therapy for at least 12 weeks to await resolution. Patients can be reassured and given appropriate advice in order to minimise these problems. Specific problems such as breast tenderness may require the use of gammalinoleic acid. Nausea and dyspepsia with oral preparations may be alleviated by adjusting the timing of the dose or taking with food; lactose sensitivity should be considered.

If problems persist beyond 12 weeks, the options to consider are reduction in dose, change of route of delivery or type of oestrogen administered.

PROGESTOGEN-RELATED ADVERSE EFFECTS

These are fluid retention, breast tenderness, headaches or migraine, mood swings, depression, acne, lower abdominal pain and backache. They occur in a cyclic pattern during the progestogen phase. They are a common cause of discontinuation. The options to consider are reduction in dose or frequency, change of route of delivery or type of oestrogen administered. Continuous combined therapy may reduce progestogenic adverse effects but is only suitable for postmenopausal women. It is important to emphasise to women the need for progestogens to reduce the risk of endometrial neoplasia.

WEIGHT GAIN

Many women decline HRT or stop therapy due to their fear of weight gain. Irrespective of HRT, women tend to gain weight with age and this begins at or near the menopause. Additionally, fat distribution changes independently of weight gain. Postmenopausally body fat assumes an android rather than a gynaecoid distribution with redistribution from hips and thighs to abdomen.

A recent Cochrane systematic review (Norman et al. 2000) has evaluated all randomised, placebo or no treatment controlled trials that detailed the effect of HRT on weight or body fat distribution. No statistically significant difference was found in mean weight gain between those using unopposed oestrogen and non-HRT users (0.66 kg, 95% CI −0.62, 1.93). No significant difference was found in mean weight gain between those using oestrogen/progestogen therapy and non-HRT users (−0.47 kg, 95% CI −1.63, 0.69). Insufficient data exist to enable meta-analysis of the effect of unopposed oestrogen on BMI. The reviewers found no statistically significant difference in mean BMI increase between those using oestrogen/progestogen and non-HRT users (−0.50, 95% CI −1.06, 0.06). Thus there is evidence of no effect from unopposed oestrogen or combined oestrogen on body weight, indicating that these regimens do not cause extra weight gain in addition to that normally gained at menopause. There is no evidence of a preventive effect of HRT on weight gain or increase in BMI associated with menopause. Insufficient evidence currently exists to enable examination of the effect of HRT on the redistribution of body fat from the hips and thighs to the abdomen that is associated with the menopause.

BLEEDING

This is a common reason for stopping HRT and it is not surprising that there is an increased use of HRT in hysterectomised women.

Monthly sequential regimens

If withdrawal bleeding is heavy or prolonged or there is breakthrough bleeding, the dose and type of progestogen need to be altered. Pelvic pathology will need exclusion if the problem is persistent or does not respond to treatment. Conversely, women are often concerned if they do not have withdrawal bleeds with monthly sequential HRT. This occurs in about five percent of women and reflects endometrial atrophy and is not an indication for endometrial biopsy. However, in women with premature ovarian failure the possibility of pregnancy should be borne in mind.

Long-cycle HRT regimens
Breakthrough bleeding is common in the first three to six months of therapy but thereafter needs assessment.

'No bleed' therapy
With continuous combined therapies or tibolone it is not unusual for women to bleed during the first six months of therapy, and in most cases it is light bleeding or spotting. The frequency of bleeding decreases over time and at 12 months most women are amenorrhoeic. The amenorrhoea rates differ with the various regimens and the ratio of oestrogen to progestogen. Increasing the proportion of progestogen reduces bleeding. For some women the ratio has to be specifically tailored. With regard to tibolone the amenorrhoea rate at one year is similar to continuous combined therapy, but there are fewer bleeding episodes in the initial months. The incidence of bleeding is lower, the longer the woman has been postmenopausal. Investigation needs to be undertaken if bleeding persists beyond six months of therapy or occurs after many months of amenorrhoea.

VASOMOTOR SYMPTOM CONTROL USING NON-OESTROGEN-BASED THERAPY
Some women do not wish to take oestrogens to deal with vasomotor symptoms and the following options are available.

- **Clonidine:** classically 50–75mg twice daily has been used but it is of limited value and effectiveness.

- **Progestogens** such as norethisterone 5 mg/day or megestrol acetate 40 mg/day can be effective in controlling hot flushes and night sweats. In such doses norethisterone affords some protection to the skeleton, but there are no data at present regarding megestrol acetate. It must be remembered that progestogens used in non-contraceptive doses increase the risk of venous thromboembolism in the same way as HRT.

- **Propanolol** is now little used because studies of its effects have produced conflicting results.

References

Norman, R.J., Flight, I.H. and Rees, M.C. (2000) Oestrogen and progestogen hormone replacement therapy for peri-menopausal and post-menopausal women: weight and body fat distribution. *Cochrane Database Syst Rev* **2**, CD001018.

Ross, R.K., Paganini-Hill, A., Wan, P.C. *et al.* (2000) Effect of hormone replacement therapy on breast cancer risk: estrogen versus estrogen plus progestin. *J Natl Cancer Inst* **92**, 328–32.

Schairer, C., Lubin, J., Troisi, R. *et al.* (2000) Menopausal estrogen and estrogen-progestin replacement therapy and breast cancer risk. *JAMA* **283**, 485–91.

7 Specific pre-existing medical conditions and HRT

Women wishing to take HRT may have a pre-existing medical condition, which data sheets may list as a contraindication to therapy. However, there is usually little supporting evidence and women may be unnecessarily denied therapy. Furthermore, this may lead to underprescribing of HRT in groups such as diabetics who potentially may benefit significantly. In women at increased risk of osteoporosis, bone mineral density will need to be monitored (see Chapter 3). This chapter is a pragmatic view based on evidence where available, and on expert opinion where not, on HRT-prescribing in specific conditions.

Cardiovascular disease

HYPERTENSION

There is no evidence that HRT elevates blood pressure or has an adverse effect in women with hypertension. Rarely, conjugated equine oestrogens cause severe hypertension, but this returns to normal when treatment is stopped.

VALVULAR HEART DISEASE

HRT is not contraindicated in women with valvular heart disease. In women taking anticoagulants there may be more problems, with irregular or heavy bleeding requiring an adjustment of the dose of progestogen relative to that of the oestrogen. Should endometrial biopsy be required, antibiotic therapy needs to be instigated.

CORONARY HEART DISEASE

This controversial area is covered in Chapter 4.

CEREBROVASCULAR ACCIDENT

There is little evidence that either supports or refutes the use of HRT in such women.

VENOUS THROMBOEMBOLISM

This subject is covered in Chapter 5. Women with a personal or family history of venous thromboembolism are best managed in conjunction with haematologists.

HYPERLIPIDAEMIA

In women the most significant lipid risk factors are HDL (high density lipoprotein), triglyceride and Lp(a). The increased risk associated with raised triglyceride and LDL (low density lipoprotein) can be offset by elevated HDL. In terms of lipids, the ideal HRT would increase HDL without increasing triglyceride, decrease LDL cholesterol and Lp(a). The effects depend on the type of steroid and the route of administration. Oral oestrogen reduces Lp(a) and LDL and increases HDL and triglycerides. The transdermal route is less effective at reducing Lp(a) and LDL but does not increase triglyceride or HDL. The type of progestogen is also important. Oral HRT with a non-androgenic progestogen will increase HDL, decrease LDL, Lp(a) and increase triglyceride. Oral HRT with a 19-nortestosterone derivative will decrease LDL, Lp(a) but will not increase HDL and be neutral for triglyceride. Thus HRT in these women needs to be tailored to their lipid profile: for example, in women with hypertriglyceridaemia the transdermal is preferred to the oral route. HRT can be combined with statins.

Raloxifene and tamoxifen reduce total cholesterol and LDL while remaining neutral towards triglyceride and HDL. Although much discussed, as yet there is no randomised controlled trial evidence available for SERMs for cardiovascular events. A large randomised controlled trial of the effects of raloxifene on cardiovascular endpoints is currently under way.

Neurological disease

MIGRAINE

This condition is more common in women than in men and is usually a condition of the reproductive years starting during the teens and twenties. It is unusual for migraines to start after the age of 50 years. Menstruation is often a significant trigger. Migraine often improves after a natural menopause, but may be worsened after bilateral oophorectomy if HRT is not given. There is no good evidence to support the idea that HRT aggravates migraine. Since migraine can be triggered by fluctuating oestrogen concentrations, the transdermal route is favoured over the oral one, because it produces more stable levels. Too high an oestrogen dose can trigger migraine aura, which usually resolves as the dose is reduced. Unlike the contraceptive pill, there are no data to suggest that the risk of ischaemic stroke is increased in women with migraine with aura taking HRT. Sequential progestogen therapy may be a trigger for migraine. The strategies that can be employed are changing the type of progestogen (19-nortestosterone to 17-hydroxyprogesterone derivatives), changing to continuous combined therapy, delivering the progestogen transdermally or into the uterus using the levonorgestrel device.

EPILEPSY

The data regarding HRT and the menopause and epilepsy are limited. The number of patients is small and the type and dose of HRT have not been systematically examined. It is a concern that some anti-epileptics are liver enzyme inducers; however, there are no data yet as to whether the transdermal is preferable to the oral route. It is also not known whether these women taking oral therapy should take an increased dose, extrapolating from combined oral contraceptives. Furthermore, there are data to suggest that anticonvulsant therapy causes changes in calcium and bone metabolism and may lead to decreased bone mass with the risk of osteoporotic fractures. The two widely used antiepileptic drugs, phenytoin and carbamazepine, are recognised to have direct effects on bone cells, leading to impaired bone formation.

PARKINSON'S DISEASE

Epidemiological studies associate postmenopausal oestrogen use with a reduction in risk of Parkinson's disease. In animal models, oestrogens have been shown to attenuate neuronal death in rodent models of Parkinson's disease. The evidence again regarding acute effects of HRT and Parkinson's disease are again limited. Transdermal 17β-oestradiol therapy appears to display a slight prodopaminergic (or antiparkinsonian) effect without consistently altering dyskinesias. It would therefore seem that HRT use is not contraindicated.

ALZHEIMER'S DISEASE

This area is covered in Chapter 4. Currently there is no good evidence that HRT will help women with established disease.

Gastrointestinal tract

GALLBLADDER DISEASE

The data on the effect of HRT on cholelithiasis are limited. A recent (Hulley *et al.* 1998) randomised placebo-controlled trial of oral HRT in elderly women for the secondary prevention of cardiovascular disease has shown an increased incidence of gallbladder disease. As a confounder, women receiving HRT may have pre-existing silent disease. It is usually recommended that in women with pre-existing disease the non-oral route should be used, but there is little evidence to support this.

LIVER DISEASE

It is advisable to use a non-oral route of oestrogen therapy. Treating such women should be undertaken in collaboration with the gastroenterologists, and liver function should be monitored.

CROHN'S DISEASE

A major consideration in such women is the increased risk of osteoporosis, which may result either from the disease itself or long-term use of corticosteroids. The transdermal route of HRT is usually preferred to ensure adequate absorption.

Endocrine

DIABETES MELLITUS

The prevalence of non-insulin-dependent diabetes mellitus is increasing in postmenopausal women. The condition raises the risk of developing coronary heart disease. Until recently data sheets for HRT and its section in the *British National Formulary* both advised caution when using HRT in women with diabetes. This resulted in women with diabetes being up to 50% less likely to be prescribed HRT than non-diabetics. There is now emerging evidence that oestrogen improves insulin sensitivity, dysplidemia and fibrinolysis, and may improve endothelial dysfunction with no apparent adverse effect on blood pressure or body weight. In 2000 the North American Menopause Society provided a consensus statement on the management of women with diabetes. The statement indicated that the greatest benefits may be obtained from the use of transdermal oestrogen preparations or low doses of oral 17β–oestradiol rather than conjugated equine oestrogens, especially with regard to improvement in dyslipidaemia and the threat of oestrogen-induced hypertriglyceridaemia. The choice of progestogen is less clear but micronised progesterone or dydrogesterone would appear to have the least adverse effect on insulin sensitivity and HDL cholesterol concentration. Glucose levels should be monitored closely and insulin dose adjusted, if necessary. Osteoporosis is also an issue in women with insulin-dependent diabetes, since they have a lower bone mineral density in middle age than both non-diabetic individuals and those with non-insulin-dependent diabetes. Clearly more research is required.

THYROID DISEASE

A past history of hyperthyroidism of any aetiology is associated with an increased risk of osteoporosis and hip fracture. This effect is found mainly in the short rather than long term. This may result from either endogenous overproduction of thyroxine or over-replacement in hypothyroidism. Patients presenting with hyperthyroidism should be screened for osteoporosis. Thyroxine replacement should be adjusted so that thyroid-stimulating hormone (TSH) is not suppressed. Thyroxine replacement therapy in patients with suppressed TSH levels increases postmenopausal bone loss. Thyroid replacement is not a contraindication for HRT.

Pelvic disorders

LEIOMYOMAS

These are oestrogen-dependent tumours that tend to shrink after the menopause. Shrinkage may be prevented or enlargement may occur with HRT and cause heavy or painful withdrawal bleeds or irregular bleeding. The evidence of the effect of different types of HRT on fibroid growth is poor. Ultrasound examinations may be helpful in documenting the fibroids, and regular pelvic examinations are recommended at six-monthly intervals, initially and annually thereafter if there is no marked increase in size.

ENDOMETRIOSIS

This is an oestrogen-sensitive condition leading to a reluctance to prescribe HRT. Theoretically, oestrogen therapy can reactivate the disease, even where there has been apparent surgical removal of all the endometriotic tissue. The risks, however, appear to be small. Nearly all studies show no adverse effect of addback therapy on the effectiveness of gonadotrophin-releasing hormone (GnRH) analogues. Patients with a history of endometriosis may be at particular risk of osteoporosis, either as a consequence of either repeated course of GnRH analogues or as a result of bilateral oophorectomy. Some gynaecologists avoid starting oestrogen-based HRT for the first six months after oophorectomy, giving a progestogen-only, continuous combined therapy or tibolone to control vasomotor symptoms, where there was extensive disease. There is no good evidence base to recommend whether an unopposed, an opposed continuous combined regimen or tibolone should be used. Management of potential recurrence is best monitored by responding to the recurrence of symptoms.

OVARIAN AND CERVICAL CANCER

These are not oestrogen-dependent malignancies. However, this statement may not pertain to endometrioid ovarian malignancies, and oestrogen here should be used with caution. The association of postmenopausal HRT with ovarian cancer is not established. Some studies have recorded no increase, no association or increased risk. More recent case–control studies have suggested an increased risk, especially in the very long term. This issue is unresolved and requires further examination.

Breast disease

BENIGN BREAST DISEASE

The exact effect of HRT on mastalgia and benign breast disease is still poorly defined. The rate of mastalgia on starting HRT is quite high, occurring in up to 40% of women. However, it usually reduces as treatment is continued. HRT use and risk of benign proliferative epithelial disorders of the breast (BPED) has been examined in a large study in Canada. In postmenopausal women, there was a positive association between duration of HRT use and risk of BPED, the adjusted incidence rate ratio (95% CI) in those who had used HRT for more than eight years being 1.70 (1.06–2.72).

Another study has examined the invasive breast carcinoma risk associated with oestrogen replacement therapy in women with histories of histologically defined breast lesions. This was a retrospective long-term cohort study of a consecutive series of women who underwent breast biopsies that proved to be benign between 1952 and 1978. HRT did not significantly elevate the risk of invasive breast carcinoma in women with previous histologically defined benign breast disease.

Autoimmune disease

RHEUMATOID ARTHRITIS

This is a systemic disorder that manifests primarily as a chronic, inflammatory polyarthropathy. It is six times more common in the sixth decade than the second, and women are affected approximately 2.5 times more frequently than men. Women with rheumatoid arthritis are at increased risk of osteoporosis. This is related to steroid use and the immobility caused by the disease. Furthermore, bone resorption is increased in rheumatoid arthritis and this is related to disease activity. There is no evidence that the use of HRT affects the risk of developing rheumatoid arthritis, nor that it induces flares in menopausal women.

SYSTEMIC LUPUS ERYTHEMATOSUS

This is a rare rheumatic disease characterised by fever, arthritis, pleuropericarditis, skin rashes, grand mal seizures, kidney failure or pancytopenia, which characteristically flares during pregnancy. The increased life expectancy of lupus patients means that early cardiovascular mortality and glucocorticoid-associated bone loss are now important issues. Surveys have found fractures occurring in 12.3% of lupus patients. There is nearly a five-fold increase in fracture occurrence in the women with lupus compared with women from the US population. Older age at lupus diagnosis and longer use of corticosteroids were associated with time from lupus diagnosis to fracture.

HRT is an ideal candidate therapy in postmenopausal lupus patients, given its benefits on prevention of osteoporosis in the general population. However, physicians are reluctant to prescribe HRT in menopausal lupus patients because SLE is a purported oestrogen-dependent disease. The sparse available evidence does not show that it increases lupus flare rate. However, in women with lupus and a previous venous thromboembolism or positive for lupus anticoagulant, HRT should be considered with caution.

Other

OTOSCLEROSIS

This condition is inherited as a Mendelian dominant characteristic, leading to progressive deafness. There is evidence that pregnancy can aggravate it, and it can rarely worsen with oral contraceptives. However, there are no data to support the suggestion that HRT causes a deterioration of the disease. Since the natural course of the disease is progressive, it is likely that hearing will become more impaired in long-term HRT users.

MALIGNANT MELANOMA

This is a controversial area. It is generally accepted that there is no association between the risk of melanoma and use of HRT. Reports of melanoma prognosis and HRT are contradictory. Oestrogen receptors are present on melanomas, but it unlikely that oestradiol has a direct effect on melanogenesis. Lentigo maligna is the precursor of lentigo maligna melanoma. It is most common in the eighth decade, found on the cheek or neck and closely correlated to ultraviolet radiation exposure. The possession of both oestrogen and progesterone receptors by lentigo maligna suggests a possible role of these steroids in malignant transformation.

TRANSPLANT

Bone mass is reduced in a high percentage of patients following organ or marrow transplantation with the prevalence of osteopenia or osteoporosis reported to be as high as 80%. Up to 65% of transplant recipients will experience an osteoporosis-related fracture and the likelihood of developing such a serious outcome is dependent on pre-existing disease and immunosuppressive therapy. Post-transplant glucocorticoid therapy plays a major role in the further reduction in bone mass observed in these patients. The additional role of other immunosuppressant treatments in bone loss is less clear but there is some evidence to suggest that cyclosporin A (CsA) and (tacrolimus) FK506 result in high bone turnover osteopenia. HRT should be considered in transplant survivors along with other anti-osteoporotic strategies. However, the data are limited.

RENAL FAILURE

Patients with end-stage renal disease are at increased risk for early menopause, osteoporosis, cognitive dysfunction and cardiovascular disease. However, it is a concern that few postmenopausal women with renal failure receive HRT. Data are also needed in this population to define the benefits of HRT.

References

Hulley, S., Grady, D., Bush, T. *et al.* (1998) Randomized trial of estrogen plus progestin for secondary prevention of coronary heart disease in postmenopausal women. Heart and Estrogen/progestin Replacement Study (HERS) Research Group. *JAMA* **280**, 605–13.

North American Menopause Society (2000) Effects of menopause and estrogen replacement therapy or hormone replacement therapy in women with diabetes mellitus: consensus opinion of the North American Menopause Society. *Menopause* **7**, 87–95.

8 Monitoring HRT

This chapter covers the issues of patient assessment and follow-up, concordance with therapy and contraception.

Patient assessment

To obtain the long-term benefits of HRT it is recommended that women continue with therapy long-term, since the benefits of treatment cease when therapy is stopped. However, there is controversy about the frequency of follow-up and what examinations should be undertaken. A wide range of recommendations for monitoring and suggestions for the frequency of follow-up is provided by the data sheets of the various HRT preparations. These recommendations are almost certainly written with the main aim of preventing litigation. There are no randomised controlled trials. The vast majority of monitoring occurs in primary rather than in secondary care. The purpose of some of the follow-up visits is to deal with adverse effects, which are a major reason for discontinuation of HRT.

It would be prudent to undertake an initial patient assessment with discussion of the endpoints of treatment before starting therapy. The next review could be at three months to determine whether the HRT preparation is suitable and controlling menopausal symptoms. Thereafter women could be seen six-monthly or annually. Some experts recommend measuring blood pressure at each visit, undertaking pelvic and breast examination every 12–18 months, but this is not evidence-based. The Committee on Safety of Medicines (CSM) advised in March 2001 that clinical examination of the breasts and pelvic examination is not routinely necessary in all women taking HRT, but should be performed if clinically indicated. These recommendations are in line with those for women taking the oral contraceptive pill.

INITIAL PATIENT ASSESSMENT

This should include menopausal status, gynaecological and general medical history, with use of concomitant medications. Family history with special emphasis on cardiovascular disease, osteoporosis, venous thrombo-embolism, breast cancer and ovarian cancer should be elicited. The benefits and risks of HRT need to be discussed, as well as potential duration of therapy. It is usually recommended that physical examination should include height and weight, blood pressure estimation, breast palpation and a speculum and bimanual pelvic examination (see above).

FOLLOW-UP ASSESSMENT

Blood pressure monitoring

On average blood pressure does not change with HRT and this has been confirmed in randomised placebo-controlled trials. On rare occasions conjugated equine oestrogens cause severe hypertension but this returns to normal when treatment is stopped. In patients with pre-existing hypertension oestrogens can be given safely, but blood pressure should be monitored regularly at six-monthly intervals or more frequently if control is poor, as would be good clinical practice in any patient with hypertension. There is no evidence that HRT has an adverse effect on blood pressure in hypertensive women.

Bleeding patterns

Irregular bleeding or heavier withdrawal bleeding should always be taken seriously and is an indication for pelvic examination and investigation (see Chapter 3). It must be remembered that vaginal ultrasound cannot be used to replace endometrial biopsy. Studies have shown little association between endometrial thickness measured by transvaginal ultrasonography and endometrial pathology. Ultrasound is useful for detection of other pelvic pathology such as fibroids and ovarian cysts.

In addition, the timing of the bleed during sequential oestrogen/progestogen regimens does not give any guide to the state of the endometrium.

BREAST EXAMINATION AND MAMMOGRAPHY

Breast self-examination and breast awareness

The role of breast self-examination is controversial and there are no specific data for women taking HRT. Self-examination is a systematic method of self-inspection and palpation of the breast performed by a woman at the same stage each month (preferably following menstruation). In the general population it does not appear to reduce mortality from breast cancer and it may increase anxiety.

Breast awareness involves a woman being aware of what is normal for her regarding the look and feel of her breasts throughout her menstrual cycle. Again there are no data with regard to women taking HRT.

Breast palpation

Conflicting advice has been given in the UK by the government authorities. In February 1998 a circular was issued by the Department of Health that detailed the lack of evidence to support the practice of breast palpation as a screening procedure in the well woman. It recommended that women should be taught breast awareness and encouraged to attend for three-yearly mammography screens after the age of 50 years. The Committee advised that breast palpation should not be included as part of routine health screening and should not be delegated to a primary care nurse.

In May 1998 the situation became confused when a further circular from the Department of Health (CMO's Update 18) highlighted the conflict between the advice given in February 1998 and the statement from manufacturers of HRT that breast examination should be carried out in women on starting such treatment and periodically afterwards. The Department of Health then concluded that the frequency of breast examinations should follow manufacturers' advice at present. In May 2000 the CSM advised that it is unnecessary for women taking oral contraceptives to have routine breast examination.

In March 2001 the CSM advised that clinical examination of the breasts is not routinely necessary in all women taking HRT, but should be performed if clinically indicated. Assessment of clinical indication should be based on personal and family history. The CSM advised that breast screening by mammography has higher sensitivity and specificity than clinical breast examination. Therefore, women on HRT should be encouraged to participate in the national breast cancer screening programme, which invites all women aged 50–64 years for mammography every three years. Women over the age of 64 years are eligible for free three-yearly screening on request. The CSM agreed that breast awareness should be encouraged, as most breast cancers that are not found on mammography are found by women themselves.

Mammography

Policies regarding mammography vary from country to country. In the UK there is a national screening programme between the ages of 50 and 64 years, with three-yearly mammograms. Starting HRT is not considered an indication for a baseline mammogram. In women under the age of 50 years mammography should be offered to those who have significant risk factors for breast cancer such as a first-degree relative with premenopausal breast cancer. UK policy states that beyond the age of 64 years women can continue with mammography at their request, although the effectiveness is disputed.

The use of HRT can lead to various changes, including mammographic density, and may reduce the sensitivity of screening. Most increases in density occur in the first year of treatment. The effect of different regimens (oestrogen-only, oestrogen with monthly sequential progestogen, continuous combined therapy) varies in individual studies. The effect of different doses and types of oestrogen and progestogen needs to be examined. Further study of the magnitude and meaning of increased mammographic density due to the use of HRT is required.

Concordance with therapy

One of the reasons for monitoring HRT is to aid concordance with therapy. The term 'concordance' is now largely replacing 'compliance'. It shifts the emphasis away from the idea of the patient purely accepting the doctor's treatment advice and introduces the concept of informed discussion of the different treatment options. There are many reasons why women elect to take HRT or not. The frequency of HRT use in different populations varies greatly. In Western Europe rates vary between 3% and 44%. In most the percentage is below 20. Ethnic differences in HRT use have been noted with for example a lower rate of use in non-white women in the UK: uptake of other preventive health measures is also lower in these groups. Over 50% of women will have stopped therapy after one year. This is even found in women with low bone mineral density who are advised to take HRT.

Poor concordance is not limited to HRT. A study of hypertensive patients showed that 50–60% had discontinued therapy by six months and that adverse effects were an important issue. A study examining compliance with treatment for tuberculosis in hospital workers found that, at six months, 26% of doctors and 52% of other hospital workers failed to complete the course.

The majority of women take HRT for the relief of vasomotor symptoms. The prevention of osteoporosis is a less important issue. Compliance is greater in female gynaecologists or general practitioners and the spouses of their male counterparts, suggesting that good information and a positive attitude to therapy are important. Women receive much of their information from the media, resulting in incomplete understanding of the issues. Scares about the risks and adverse effects of HRT will obtain more publicity than any studies showing benefits. Furthermore, a number of studies (see for example Newton *et al.* 2001) have reported that a major reason for taking HRT was a positive attitude and recommendation by the physician. The gender of the doctor is also an important factor, with noncompliance being greater with male than with female practitioners. Concordance is greater in women following hysterectomy and bilateral oophorectomy: this could be because these women often have severe vasomotor symptoms on stopping therapy, have no vaginal bleeding and no progestogenic adverse effects.

Studies that have examined the reasons as to why women stop therapy emphasise the dislike of continued menstruation, adverse effects, lack of efficacy and concerns about long-term risks. Some women consider HRT to be unnatural and, in those with no symptoms or at low risk for osteoporosis, the benefits of therapy are limited since they do not have a problem that will respond (e.g. hot flushes).

HOW TO IMPROVE CONCORDANCE

Various strategies can be employed to improve concordance and the following are based on those from the North American Menopause Society. They will usually require several consultations and in primary care often involve the practice nurse.

- **Involvement of the woman in the decision-making process.** This may seem obvious, but is often not undertaken in a clinical situation with time constraints.

- **Clear and personalised explanation of the benefits, risks and duration of therapy.** As a result of such counselling, asymptomatic women at low risk of osteoporosis may elect not to take treatment. Also, unrealistic expectations about the results of therapy (some consider HRT to be a universal panacea) should be discussed. For women electing to take HRT for vasomotor symptom control, treatment is usually short-term, with up to five years' use on average. However, those with low bone mineral density are considering long-term therapy starting initially with HRT, with a possibility of switching over to a bisphosphonate. Uncertainties about benefits such as is current with regard to cardiovascular disease need to be explained, as well as the risks of breast cancer and VTE. These should be documented in the case record, which is helpful not only if the issues have to be discussed at a later date when new evidence is available but also to prevent litigation.

- **Discussion of the woman's preferences and which regimen she wishes to use.** This discussion will encompass the route of therapy and induced bleeding patterns. Women often complain that they were not aware of the alternative treatments available. It is helpful to show packets of medication and to give samples of placebo patches or gels to see if the patient finds them suitable. Some packaging or delivery systems may be difficult for women with limited mobility or manual dexterity to use.

- **Provide written information.** Various leaflets and videos are available from national organisations and the pharmaceutical industry, which can be useful since there is much information to be imparted.

- **Follow-up.** As previously discussed, the follow-up visits are to discuss whether therapy is suitable and medication is taken regularly.

Contraception

Contraception is an important issue for perimenopausal women, and pregnancies and births have been documented in women in their 50s. High maternal age is a significant risk factor for spontaneous abortion, ectopic pregnancy and stillbirth. There is an increasing risk of fetal malformation, with a rise in chromosomal disorders.

The normal recommendation is to continue contraception after the final menstrual period for at least two years if the woman is under 50 years and at least one year if she is over 50 years old. The final menstrual period can only be identified retrospectively and may be difficult to identify in women using a contraceptive method that renders them amenorrhoeic (intramuscular, subdermal and intrauterine progestogens), or those taking a combined oral contraceptive or monthly sequential HRT. Women who do not smoke, are normotensive and not overweight and with a benign family history, can continue low-dose combined pills until at least their mid-40s or early 50s. However, synthetic oestrogens may potentiate the age-related increase in cardio- and cerebrovascular disease. The use of progestogen-only contraception, intramuscular or subdermal progestogens with HRT has not been fully evaluated. 'Natural' methods will become unreliable as cycle length varies. Elevated FSH levels after stopping oral contraceptives or HRT may not reliably indicate infertility.

SUITABLE CONTRACEPTIVE OPTIONS IN THE PERIMENOPAUSE

- **Non-hormonal:** Coitus interruptus, barrier*, condoms, diaphragm, spermicides, intrauterine devices, sterilisation (male or female).
- **Hormonal:** Intrauterine progestogens, combined oral contraception, progestogen-only pills, intramuscular progestogens, subdermal progestogens.

*Some vaginal preparations, including oestrogen creams and pessaries, may damage the rubber used in condoms and diaphragms, leading to increased risk of rupture.

References

Department of Health (1998) *Clinical Examination of the Breast. PL/CNO/98/1. Government's Advisory Committee on Breast Cancer Screening.* London: DoH.

Newton, K.M., LaCroix, A.Z., Buist, D.S., Anderson, L.A. and Delaney, K. (2001) What factors account for hormone replacement therapy prescribing frequency? *Maturitas* **39**, 1–10.

Sturdee, D.W., Barlow, D.H., Ulrich, L.G., Anderson, *et al.* Is the timing of withdrawal bleeding a guide to endometrial safety during sequential oestrogen-progestogen replacement therapy? *Lancet* (1994) **344**, 979–82.

9 Non-hormone replacement therapy and osteoporosis

Non-hormone replacement therapy options for the prevention and treatment of osteoporosis should be considered for women

- who do not wish to take oestrogen-based HRT
- who have a contraindication for therapy
- whose only endpoint of treatment is skeletal protection.

All the therapies must be considered in the light of their potential benefits and adverse effects profile. For some therapies, the effects of combining with HRT have been studied. Others such as intermittent use of parathyroid hormone are likely to become available soon.

Calcium salts

Calcium is the most important nutritional factor in osteoporosis. Some 99% of total body calcium is located in the skeleton and a form of calcium phosphate makes up about 65% of bone by weight. Balance studies in premenopausal women have shown that mean calcium intake at which absorbed and urinary calcium are equal is 520 mg. However, there is good evidence of an additional insensible loss of calcium through the skin, which increases the requirement to 700 mg and implies an allowance of about 900 mg. The evidence that oestrogen deficiency increases requirement has been demonstrated in calcium balance studies across the menopause. These studies show a decrease in absorption and an increase in urinary calcium excretion at the menopause. An appropriate allowance would perhaps be 1100–1200 mg.

The most rigorous situation to test the effect of calcium salts is after oophorectomy, where placebo-controlled studies show that high doses of calcium reduce bone loss. The effect of calcium appears to be due to a reduction in bone turnover.

Epidemiological studies have conflicting results, with some showing that a high dietary intake reduces risk of osteoporotic fracture and others showing an increased risk. However, women who have a high dietary intake of calcium differ from those who do not in terms of general health, education and other possibly confounding factors. Such studies have to be distinguished from those that examine the pharmacological use of calcium. Here vertebral fracture risk is reduced by about 30–40%. The data for hip fracture are more limited, but benefits have also been observed.

Most studies show that about 1.5 g of elemental calcium is necessary to preserve bone health in postmenopausal women and the elderly. This figure has been reinforced (NIH, 1994), although current UK recommendations of 700 mg/day are unlikely to change. It must be noted however that while this benefit has been found in elderly women there is no evidence that calcium on its own is capable of reversing bone loss in the perimenopause.

Calcium and vitamin D

This combination may be particularly relevant to populations in northern latitudes such as the UK, where there is much evidence of vitamin D insufficiency, especially in the elderly. In northern latitudes the cutaneous synthesis of vitamin D occurs only in summer months, and in the UK the national diet lacks sufficient amounts of this vitamin for adequate intake in the absence of solar exposure. Other more southerly countries, such as the USA, fortify foods by adding vitamin D to dairy products.

In the USA a significant reduction in long bone fractures was found in adults aged 65 years and over taking an additional 500 mg of elemental calcium and 700 iu of vitamin D daily. This study, which was double-blinded and placebo-controlled, recorded the incidence of falls, which was no different between the two groups. An earlier French study had shown a 30% lower risk of hip fracture in elderly women given 1.2 g of elemental calcium and 800 iu of vitamin D. There was also a significant reduction in all long bone fractures in women treated for 18 months. The benefits of vitamin D alone are less clear and the evidence is conflicting.

Thus in countries where both calcium and vitamin D intake is commonly below what is recommended for bone health, both supplements could confer benefits, especially in the elderly.

Bisphosphonates

Several bisphosphonates such as etidronate, alendronate, risedronate, clodronate and pamidronate have been used, mainly in the field of Paget's disease and the hypercalcaemia of malignancy. The first three are used in the prevention and treatment of osteoporosis, and also corticosteroid-induced osteoporosis. Others under investigation include ibandronate and neridronate. All bisphosphonates are poorly absorbed from the gastrointestinal tract and must be given on an empty stomach. Food or calcium-containing drinks (except water) inhibit the absorption, which at best is only 5–10% of the administered dose. Thus they must be administered in the fasting state. An adverse effect of all bisphophonates is irritation of the upper gastrointestinal tract. Symptoms resolve quickly after drug withdrawal.

Historically bisphophonates are linked to inorganic pyrophosphates. Inorganic pyrophosphate is a polyphosphate, a member of a family of compounds characterised by the presence of at least one phosphorus-oxygen-phosphorus (POP) bridge. These agents were first used to prevent calcium carbonate precipitation in water. Replacement of the POP bond with a phosphorus-carbon-phosphorus (PCP) bond, results in a stable compound resistant to degradation by pyrophosphatases, which occur *in vivo*. Bisphosphonates become incorporated into bone at sites of mineralisation and in resorption cavities. They also diffuse into osteoclasts and promote apoptosis, thus inhibiting bone resorption. High doses of bisphosphonates can also inhibit bone formation and mineralisation but for most bisphosphonates there is a wide margin of safety between a dose that blocks resorption and one that inhibits formation.

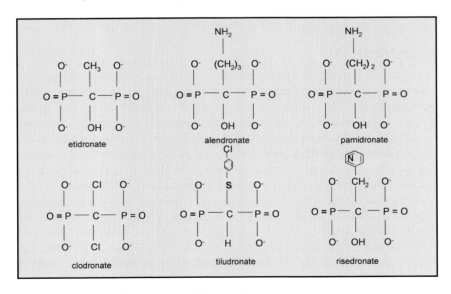

Figure 9.1 Chemical structure of bisphophonates

ETIDRONATE

Etidronate has been widely investigated in postmenopausal osteoporosis. The concentration at which etidronate inhibits bone resorption is little lower than that which inhibits bone formation. The use of high-dose etidronate results in impaired mineralisation and focal osteomalacia. Thus etidronate is given intermittently (14 out of every 90 days) and 1.250 mg of calcium salts is given during the remaining 76 days. This preparation can be given indefinitely.

There are two randomised controlled trials of the effects of etidronate on fracture frequency in osteoporotic patients. Both found a decrease in vertebral fracture frequency. Double-blind placebo-controlled trials of cyclical etidronate did not have fracture incidence as a primary endpoint and were underpowered for that kind of assessment. However, studies that used calcium either alone or with vitamin D in addition to cyclical etidronate 400 mg daily for 14 days every 11–13 weeks showed improvements in bone mineral density. Lumbar spine BMD increased by about 5% compared with a 3% fall in the placebo group.

A recent retrospective study (van Staa et al. 1998) of the use of cyclical etidronate in general practice (7977 patients) has shown that the use of this bisphosphonate is associated with fewer nonvertebral hip and wrist fractures than in those not using this treatment. Furthermore, cyclical etidronate therapy also prevents bone loss in the spine and proximal femur in early postmenopausal women. When etidronate is combined with HRT, bone gain may be superior to that observed with either agent alone.

ALENDRONATE

Alendronate is an aminobisphosphonate that has a antiresorptive potency 1000 times greater than etidronate. Approximately 1% of an administered dose enters the circulation and half of this is excreted unchanged in the urine. Unlike etidronate, the antiresorptive dose is far less than the dose required to inhibit mineralisation and so it may be administered daily.

Long-term double-blind multicentre studies have shown that continuous daily doses of 10 mg or 20 mg increased bone mineral density at both the lumbar spine and hip. The changes are most marked in the first year with a plateau occurring after two to three years. Bone mass is preserved for at least one year after treatment is stopped. With regard to fracture randomised controlled trials have shown a 50% reduction in both vertebral and nonvertebral fracture. A recent study (Rossini et al. 2000) has shown that intermittent dosing is also effective at maintaining BMD at spine and hip. Alendronate can now be given with either weekly or daily dosing. Combined use of alendronate and oestrogen produce somewhat larger increases in BMD than either agent alone.

RISEDRONATE

Risedronate is a pyridinyl bisphophonate that became available in 2000 in the UK for the management of osteoporosis. In women with established osteoporosis 5 mg daily over three years reduces the incidence of new vertebral fractures by about 45% and nonvertebral fracture by about 36%. It is also effective in the prevention of corticosteroid-induced osteoporosis.

Calcitonin

Calcitonin may be given either parenterally or by nasal spray. Much of the evidence for the efficacy of calcitonin is derived from experience with the nasal spray. Calcitonin has been used for over 20 years and has not been associated with serious adverse effects. Parenteral calcitonin can cause nausea, diarrhoea and flushing, and results in the production of neutralising antibodies in some patients. Nasal calcitonin has also been shown to reduce vertebral fractures by about 30%. There is also evidence for its efficacy as an analgesic in acute vertebral fracture.

Calcitriol, alfacalcidol and related analogues

The vitamin D derivatives most widely used are calcitriol and alfacalcidol. Alfacalcidol is the synthetic analogue of calcitriol and is metabolised to the active hormone in the liver. The effects on vertebral fracture are inconsistent, and no protective effect has been shown for hip fracture.

Fluorides

Fluoride is one of the few agents that has a marked anabolic effect on the skeleton. The efficacy of fluoride regimens continues to be controversial. While vertebral bone mineral density is increased, this has not consistently been translated as a reduction in fracture risk. No protective effect has been shown on hip fracture risk.

Selective oestrogen receptor modulators

The term selective oestrogen receptor modulators or SERMs is used for compounds that possess tissue-specific oestrogen agonist and antagonist effects. The non-steroidal anti-oestrogen tamoxifen was the first SERM. It is used an adjuvant and preventive treatment for breast cancer, since it behaves as an oestrogen antagonist in that tissue. It also displays oestrogen agonist-like effects on bone and lipids. It has no licence for use in osteoporosis and its use for prevention is confined to specialist units. There are concerns about the adverse effects of tamoxifen on the endometrium, where it acts as an oestrogen and increases the risk of endometrial hyperplasia and cancer.

Raloxifene is the first SERM to be licensed for the prevention and treatment of osteoporosis-related vertebral fracture. Studies have shown that at 24 months, the mean (+/–SE) difference in the change in bone mineral density between the women receiving 60 mg of raloxifene per day and those receiving placebo was 2.4 ± 0.4% for the lumbar spine, 2.4 ± 0.4% for the total hip, and 2.0 ± 0.4% for the total body ($P < 0.001$ for all comparisons). Raloxifene reduces vertebral fracture by 30–50%, depending on dose in women with established osteoporosis. However, it does not significantly reduce the risk of nonvertebral fracture. No comparative studies of raloxifene and other treatments for osteoporosis such as HRT and bisphosphonates are currently available.

The dose is 60 mg daily and it is suitable for postmenopausal but not perimenopausal women. It is a 'no bleed' therapy, since it does not stimulate the endometrium. It also does not stimulate breast tissue. It may reduce the risk of breast cancer; however, this is currently being evaluated. Its beneficial effects on lipids are also being examined in studies with cardiovascular endpoints. Adverse effects include vasomotor flushes and calf cramps. Therefore it is not suitable for women with vasomotor symptoms. It increases the risk of venous thromboembolism to the same extent as oestrogen-based HRT.

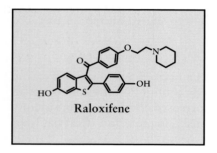

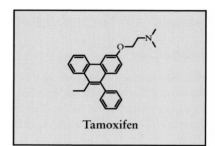

Figure 9.2 Structures of raloxifene and tamoxifen

Exercise

Animal studies have shown that bone responds to strain. Furthermore, many epidemiological studies have shown an association between the level of physical exercise and bone mass and risk of fracture. However, studies have shown a rather limited role for weight-bearing exercise in the prevention of osteoporosis at the menopause. In contrast, exercise regimens can be helpful in the management of established osteoporosis. The benefits are mainly related to increased well-being, muscle strength, postural stability and a reduction of chronic pain rather than skeletal mass. Exercise has to be carefully structured because of concerns of further fractures.

Prevention and treatment of falls

Except for vertebral fractures, the majority of fragility fractures result from falls. The risk of falling increases with age and is greater in women than in men. The importance of falls relative to the decline of bone mineral density in promoting fracture is controversial. More evidence is required about strategies to prevent falls.

HIP PROTECTORS

These are used to reduce the impact of falling directly on the hip. A randomised controlled study of hip of padded polypropylene protectors has shown a reduction of hip fracture in the treatment wing. However, hip protectors are not particularly attractive and are uncomfortable in hot weather.

References

NIH (1994) Optimal calcium intake. *JAMA* **272**, 1942–8.

Rossini M., Gatti, D., Girardello, S. *et al.* (2000) Effects of two intermittent alendronate regimens in the prevention or treatment of postmenopausal osteoporosis. *Bone* **27**, 119–22.

Van Staa, T.P., Abenhaim, L. and Cooper, C. (1998) Use of cyclical etidronate and prevention of non-vertebral fractures. *Br J Rheumatol* **37**, 87–94.

10 Complementary and alternative therapies

The evidence from randomised trials that alternative therapies improve menopausal symptoms or have the same benefits as hormone replacement therapy is poor. However, many women use them, believing them to be safer and 'more natural'. The choice of therapies is confusing. This chapter presents evidence about some of the alternative therapies currently available, with special mention for those that may interact with other therapies.

Herbalism

Herbalism needs to be used with caution in women with a contraindication to oestrogen since some herbs, e.g. ginseng, have oestrogenic properties. Furthermore, there is little control over the quality of the products; thus it is unusual to know what is actually in herbal preparations and dietary supplements. Severe adverse reactions including renal failure and cancer have been reported (Nortier et al. 2000) that were due to a manufacturing error where a nephrotoxic and carcinogenic herb was included in a Chinese herbal preparation given for weight loss. The safety of some herbs, such as aloe vera, kava and milk thistle, is being tested. Dong quai contains coumarins and can interact with anticoagulants.

BLACK COHOSH (CIMICIFUGA RACEMOSA)

This has been certified by the German commission to have a favourable risk–benefit ratio for use in 'climacteric neurovegetative complaints'. The precise mechanism of action is unclear, but some of the constituents bind to oestrogen receptors.

ST JOHN'S WORT (HYPERICUM PERFORATUM)

This can be used successfully to treat depression and has been examined in randomised controlled trials. A recent open study (Grube et al. 1999) in menopausal women in primary care showed substantial improvement in psychological and psychosomatic symptoms. Climacteric complaints diminished or disappeared completely in the majority of women. Sexual wellbeing also improved after treatment with St John's Wort extract. There are concerns that it is a liver enzyme inducer, and could potentially interact with HRT.

GINSENG

This is another popular therapy for postmenopausal women. A recent randomised, multicentre, double-blind, parallel group, placebo-controlled study (Wiklund *et al.* 1999) has been undertaken of a ginseng extract. General psychological wellbeing showed only a tendency for a slightly better overall symptomatic relief ($P < 0.1$). Subset analysis, however, reported P-values < 0.05 for depression, wellbeing and health subscales in favour of ginseng compared with placebo. No statistically significant effects were seen for vasomotor symptoms.

Phytoestrogens

Phytoestrogens are plant substances that are structurally or functionally similar to oestradiol and that are found in many foods. The preparations used vary from enriched foods such as bread and drinks (soy milk) to tablets. They consist of a number of classes, of which the lignans and isoflavones are the most important in humans. Oilseeds such as flaxseed contain the highest concentrations of lignans and they are also found in cereal bran, whole cereals, vegetables, legumes and fruits. Isoflavones occur in high concentrations in soybeans, chick peas and possibly other legumes as well as clovers. The major lignans are enterolactone and enterodiol. The major isoflavones are genistein and daidzein.

The role of phytoestrogens has stimulated considerable interest since populations consuming a diet high in isoflavones, such as the Japanese, have a lower incidence of menopausal vasomotor symptoms, cardiovascular disease, osteoporosis and of breast, colon, endometrial and ovarian cancers. Furthermore, women with breast cancer in Japan have a better prognosis than those with breast cancer in the USA or the UK. Phytoestrogens have a variety of activities: oestrogenic, anti-oestrogenic, antiviral, anti-carcinogenic, bactericidal, antifungal, anti-oxidant, anti-mutagenic, anti-hypertensive, anti-inflammatory and anti-proliferative effects. Genistein, the most extensively studied isoflavone, is an inhibitor of tyrosine kinase, DNA topoisomerases I and II and ribosomal S6 kinase. Other properties include inhibition of angiogenesis and differentiation of cancer cell lines.

Genistein and the synthetic isoflavone ipriflavone appear to maintain bone mass. In the USA the Food and Drug Administration has approved food or food substances containing specific amounts of soy protein to reduce the risk of heart disease.

Randomised placebo-controlled trials, however, are required. With regard to menopausal symptoms, the evidence is conflicting and soy seems to be no more effective than placebo. Similarly there are also debates about the effects on lipoproteins, endothelial function and blood pressure. Thus it would appear that phytoestrogens represent a group of compounds worthy of further investigation for the treatment of menopausal syndrome.

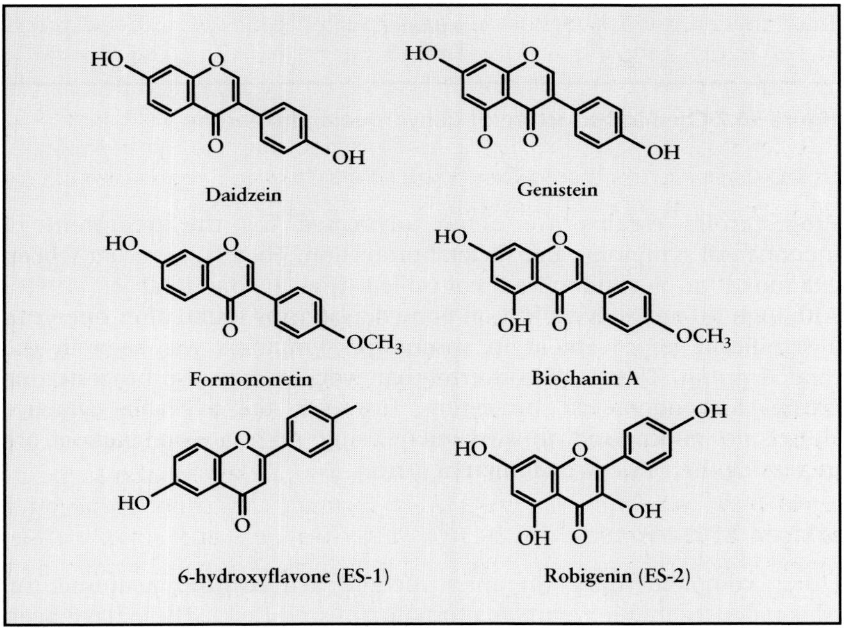

Figure 10.1 Chemical structure of some phytoestrogens

Dehydroepiandrosterone

Dehydroepiandrosterone (DHEA) is a steroid secreted by the adrenal cortex. The secretion and the blood levels of DHEA and its sulphate ester (DHEAS) decrease profoundly with age, leading to the suggestion that old age represents a DHEA deficiency syndrome and that the effects of ageing can be counteracted by DHEA 'replacement therapy'. DHEA is increasingly being used in the USA, where it is classed as a food supplement, outside medical supervision, for its supposed anti-ageing effects. Some studies have shown benefits on the skeleton, cognition, wellbeing and the vagina. The short-term effects of DHEA administration are, however, still controversial, and possible adverse effects in long-term use are, as yet, unrecorded.

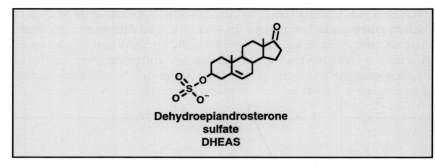

**Dehydroepiandrosterone
sulfate
DHEAS**

Figure 10.2 Chemical structure of dehydroepiandrosterone

Progesterone transdermal creams

Progesterone creams are being advocated for the treatment of menopausal symptoms and skeletal protection. They have recently been examined in a randomised controlled trial (Leonetti *et al.* 1999). Although no protective effect on bone density was found after one year, a significant improvement in vasomotor symptoms was seen in the treated group. There are concerns that women may use progesterone creams for endometrial protection. However, the available evidence shows no effect, and thus women using such a combination are increasing their risk of endometrial cancer.

Other therapies

Other complementary therapies include acupressure, acupuncture, Alexander technique, Ayurveda, osteopathy and Reiki. These have been covered in recent reviews (Zollman and Vickers 1999), and need further examination in relation to the menopause.

References

Grube, B., Walper, A. and Wheatley, D. (1999). St John's Wort extract: efficacy for menopausal symptoms of psychological origin. *Adv Ther* **16**, 177–86.

Leonetti, H.B., Longo, S. and Anasti, J.N. (1999). Transdermal progesterone cream for vasomotor symptoms and postmenopausal bone loss. *Obstet Gynecol* **94**, 225–8.

Nortier, J.L., Martinez, M.C., Schmeiser, H.H. *et al.* (2000) Urothelial carcinoma associated with the use of a Chinese herb (Aristolochia fangchi). *N Engl J Med* **342**, 1686–92.

Wiklund, I.K., Mattsson, L.A., Lindgren, R. and Limoni, C. (1999) Effects of a standardized ginseng extract on quality of life and physiological parameters in symptomatic postmenopausal women: a double-blind, placebo-controlled trial. Swedish Alternative Medicine Group. *Int J Clin Pharmacol Res* **19**, 89–99.

Zollman, C. and Vickers, A. (1999) ABC of complementary medicine. Complementary medicine in conventional practice. *Br Med J* **319**, 901–4.

Recommended reading

Chapter 1

Burger, H.G. (1996) The menopausal transition. In Barlow, D. H. (Ed): *The Menopause: The Key Issues, Bailliere's Clinical Obstetrics and Gynaecology*, Vol. 10, pp. 347–60. London: Bailliere Tindall.

Cresswell, J.L., Egger, P., Fall, C.H. *et al.* (1997) Is the age of menopause determined *in utero*? *Early Hum Dev* **49**, 143–8.

Ebbiary, N.A., Lenton, E.A. and Cooke, I.D. (1994) Hypothalamic-pituitary ageing: progressive increase in FSH and LH concentrations throughout the reproductive life in regularly menstruating women. *Clin Endocrinol* **41**, 199–206.

Gold, E.B., Bromberger, J., Crawford, S. *et al* (2001) Factors associated with age at natural menopause in a multiethnic sample of midlife women. *Am J Epidemiol;***153**, 865-74.

Kalantaridou, S.N. and Nelson, L.M. (2000) Premature ovarian failure is not premature menopause. *Ann NY Acad Sci* **900**, 393–402.

Morabia, A. and Costanza, M.C. (1998) International variability in ages at menarche, first live birth, and menopause. World Health Organization Collaborative Study of Neoplasia and Steroid Contraceptives. *Am J Epidemiol* **148**, 1195–1205.

Raven, P., Lind, C. and Nilas, L. (1995) Lack of influence of simple premenopausal hysterectomy on bone mass and bone metabolism. *Am J Obstet Gynecol* **172**, 891–5.

Seeley, A. and Ashton, S. (2000) Premature ovarian failure: a practical approach. *J Br Meno Soc* **6**, 107–9.

Seltzer, G.B., Schupf, N., Wu, H.S. (2001) A prospective study of menopause in women with Down's syndrome. *J Intellect Disabil Res* **45**, 1–7.

Siddle, N., Sarrel, P. and Whitehead, M. (1987) The effect of hysterectomy on the age at ovarian failure: identification of a subgroup of women with premature loss of ovarian function and literature review *Fertil Steril* **47**, 94–100.

Treloar, A.E., Boynton, R.E., Behn, B.G. and Brown, B.W. (1967) Variation of the human menstrual cycle through reproductive life. *Int J Fertil* **12**, 77–126.

Watson, N. R., Studd, J.W., Garnett, T., Savvas, M. and Milligan, P. (1995) Bone loss after hysterectomy with ovarian conservation. *Obstet Gynecol* **86**, 72–7.

WHO Scientific Group on research on the Menopause in the 1990s. WHO Technical Report Series 866, Geneva, Switzerland, 1994.

Chapter 2

Avis, N.E., Brambilla, D., McKinlay, S.M. and Vass, K. (1994) A longitudinal analysis of the association between menopause and depression. Results from the Massachusetts Women's Health Study. *Ann Epidemiol* **4**, 214–20.

Bebbington, P.E., Dunn, G., Jenkins, R. *et al.* (1998) The influence of age and sex on the prevalence of depressive conditions: report from the National Survey of Psychiatric Morbidity. *Psychol Med* **28**, 9–19.

Castelo Branco, C., Pons, F., Gratacos, E. *et al.* (1994) Relationship between skin collagen and bone changes during ageing. *Maturitas* **18**, 199–206.

Colditz, G.A. and Stampfer, M.J. (1992) Cardiovascular effects of the menopause and estrogen replacement: the epidemiological evidence. In: Swartz, D.P. *Hormone Replacement Therapy*. Baltimore, MD: Williams and Wilkins, pp. 109–37.

Consensus Development Conference (1993) Diagnosis, prophylaxis, and treatment of osteoporosis. *Am. J. Med* **94**, 646–50.

Dennerstein, L., Lehert, P., Dudley, E. and Guthrie, J. (2001) Factors contributing to positive mood during the menopausal transition. *J Nerv Ment Dis* **189**, 84–9.

Department of Health, National Service Framework on Older People, 2001 http://www.doh.gov.uk/nsf/olderpeople.htm.

Department of Health (1998) Quick reference primary care guide on the prevention and treatment of osteoporosis. Department of Health, PO Box 410, Wetherby LS23 7LN. www. open. gov. uk/doh/osteop. htm.

Dolan, P. and Torgerson, D.J. (1998) The cost of treating osteoporotic fractures in the United Kingdom female population. *Osteoporosis Int* **8**, 611–17.

Lock, M. and Kaufert, P. (2001) Menopause, local biologies, and cultures of aging. *Am J Human Biol* **13**, 494–504.

McCoy, N.L. (1998) Methodological problems in the study of sexuality and the menopause. *Maturitas* **29**, 51–60.

Milsom, I. and Molander, U. (1998) Urogenital ageing. *J Br Meno Soc* **4**, 151–6.

Morse, C.A., Dudley, E., Guthrie, J. and Dennerstein, L. (1998) Relationships between premenstrual complaints and perimenopausal experiences. *J Psychosom Obstet Gynaecol* **19**, 182–91.

Newton, J. (1998) The epidemiology of coronary heart disease and HRT: what are the contentious issues? *J Br Meno Soc* **4**, 135–42.

Pearlstein, T., Rosen, K. and Stone, A.B. (1997) Mood disorders and menopause. *Endocrinol Metab Clin North Am* **26**, 279–94.

Rees, M.C. and Barlow, D.H. (1988) Absence of sustained reflex vasoconstriction in women with menopausal flushes *Hum Reprod* **3**, 823–5.

Riggs, B.L. and Melton, L.J. (1986) Involutional osteoporosis. *N Engl J Med* **314**, 1676–86.

Royal College of Physicians of London. (1999) Osteoporosis. Clinical Guidelines for prevention and treatment. London: RCP.

Sernbo, I. and Johnell, O. (1993) Consequences of a hip fracture: a prospective study over 1 year. *Osteoporos Int* **3**, 148–53.

Raimond, G.V., Smolders, M. J. and van der Mooren, M.J. (2000) New emerging risk factors for cardiovascular disease. *J Br Meno Soc* **6**, 27–33.

Tang, G.W. (1994) The climacteric of Chinese factory workers. *Maturitas* **19**,77–82.

Chapter 3

Bennett, I.C., Gattas, M. and Teh, B.T. (1999) The genetic basis of breast cancer and its clinical implications. *Aust N Z J Surg* **69**, 95–105.

Boyd, N.F., Lockwood, G.A., Byng, J.W., Tritchler, D.L. and Yaffe, M.J. (1998) Mammographic densities and breast cancer risk. *Cancer Epidemiol Biomarkers Prev* **7**, 1133–44.

Department of Health (1998) Quick reference primary care guide on the prevention and treatment of osteoporosis Department of Health, PO Box 410, Wetherby LS23 7LN. www. open. gov. uk/doh/osteop.htm.

Hannon, R. and Eastell, R. (1998) Bone metabolism and osteoporosis. *J Br Meno Soc* **4**, 103–6.

Holbert, T. (1997) Transvaginal ultrasonographic measurement of endometrial thickness in postmenopausal women receiving estrogen replacement therapy. *Am J Obstet Gynecol* **176**, 1334–9.

Karlsson, B., Granberg, S., Wikland, M. *et al.* (1995) Transvaginal ultrasonography of the endometrium in women with postmenopausal bleeding – a Nordic multicenter study. *Am J Obstet Gynecol* **172**, 1488–94.

Korhonen, M.O., Symons, J.P., Hyde, B.M. Rowan, J.P. and Wilborn, W.H. (1997) Histologic classification and pathologic findings for endometrial biopsy Specimens obtained from 2964 perimenopausal and postmenopausal women undergoing screening for continuous hormones as replacement therapy (CHART 2 Study) *Am J Obstet Gynecol* **176**, 377–80.

Lynge, E. (1998) Mammography screening for breast cancer in Copenhagen April 1991. March 1997. Mammography Screening Evaluation Group. *APMIS Suppl* **83**,1–44.

Lucassen, A., Watson, E. and Eccles, D. (2001) Evidence based case report: Advice about mammography for a young woman with a family history of breast cancer. *Br Med J* **322**, 1040–42.

Peel, N. (1998) Measurement of bone mineral density. *J Br Meno Soc* **4**, 73–6.

Rutter, C.M., Mandelson, M.T., Laya, M.B., Seger, D.J. and Taplin, S. (2001) Changes in breast density associated with initiation, discontinuation, and continuing use of hormone replacement therapy. *JAMA* **285**, 171–6.

Wells, M. (1996) 'Female Genital Tract' in: J.C.E. Underwood (Ed.) *General and Systematic Pathology*, 2nd ed. Edinburgh: Churchill Livingstone, pp. 551–84.

Chapter 4

Ashcroft, G.S., Dodsworth, J., van Boxtel, E. *et al.* (1997) Estrogen accelerates cutaneous wound healing associated with an increase in TGF-betal levels. *Nat Med* **3**, 1209–15.

Baldereschi, M., Di Carlo, A., Lepore, V. *et al.* (1998) Estrogen-replacement therapy and Alzheimer's disease in the Italian Longitudinal Study on Aging. *Neurology* **50**, 996–1002.

Barrett-Connor, E. and Grady, D. (1998) Hormone replacement therapy, heart disease, and other considerations. *Annu Rev Public Health* **19**, 55–72.

Cardozo, L., Bachmann, G., McClish, D., Fonda, D. and Birgerson, L. (1998) Meta-analysis of estrogen therapy in the management of urogenital atrophy in postmenopausal women: second report of the Hormones and Urogenital Therapy Committee. *Obstet Gynecol* **92**, 722–7.

Delmas, P.D., Confavreux, E., Garnero, P. *et al.* (2000) A combination of low doses of 17 beta-estradiol and norethisterone acetate prevents bone loss and normalizes bone turnover in postmenopausal women. *Osteoporos Int* **11**, 177–87.

Eddy, D.M., Johnston, C.C., Cummings, S.R. *et al.* (1998) Osteoporosis: cost-effectiveness analysis and review of the evidence for prevention, diagnosis and treatment. *Osteoporos Int Suppl* **4**.

Grodstein, F., Colditz, G.A. and Stampfer, M.J. (1996) Post-menopausal hormone use and tooth loss: a prospective study. *J Am Den Assoc* (Suppl). **127**, 370–77.

Grodstein, F., Newcomb, P.A. and Stampfer, M.J. (1999) Postmenopausal hormone use and the risk of colorectal cancer: a review and meta-analysis. *Am J Med* **106**, 574–82.

Haskell, S.G., Richardson, E.D. and Horwitz, R.I. (1997) The effect of estrogen replacement therapy on cognitive function in women: a critical review of the literature. *J Clin Epidemiol* **50**, 1249–64.

Herrington, D.M., Reboussin, D.M., Brosnihan, K.B. *et al.* (2000) Effects of estrogen replacement on the progression of coronary-artery atherosclerosis. *N Engl J Med* **343**, 522–9.

Henderson, V.W., Paganini-Hill, A., Miller, B.L. *et al.* (2000) Estrogen for Alzheimer's disease in women: randomized, double-blind, placebo-controlled trial. *Neurology* **54**, 295–301.

Hulley, S., Grady, D., Bush, T. *et al.* (1998) Randomized trial of estrogen plus progestin for secondary prevention of coronary heart disease in postmenopausal women. Heart and Estrogen/progestin Replacement Study (HERS) Research Group. *JAMA* **280**, 605–13.

Komulainen, M.H., Kroger, H., Tuppurainen, M.T. *et al.* (1998) HRT and Vit D in prevention of non-vertebral fractures in postmenopausal women: a 5 year randomized trial. *Maturitas* **31**, 45–54.

Lane, J.M. and Nydick, M. (1999) Osteoporosis: current modes of prevention and treatment. *J Am Acad Orthop Surg* **7**, 19–31.

Lufkin, E.G., Wahner, H.W., O'Fallon, W.M. *et al.* (1992) Treatment of postmenopausal osteoporosis with transdermal estrogen. *Ann Intern Med* **117**, 1–9.

Mulnard, R.A., Cotman, C.W., Kawas, C. *et al.* (2000) Estrogen replacement therapy for treatment of mild to moderate Alzheimer disease: a randomized controlled trial. Alzheimer's Disease Cooperative Study. *JAMA* **283**, 1007–15.

Naessen, T., Lindmark, B. and Larsen, H.C. (1997) Better postural balance in elderly women receiving estrogens. *Am J Obstet Gynecol* **177**, 412–6.

Paganini-Hill, A. and Henderson, V.W. (1996) Estrogen replacement therapy and risk of Alzheimer's disease. *Arch Intern Med* **156**, 2213–17.

Petitti, D.B., Sidney, S., Quesenberry, C.P. Jr and Bernstein, A. (1998) Ischemic stroke and use of estrogen and estrogen/progestogen as hormone replacement therapy. *Stroke* **29**, 23–8.

Royal College of Physicians (1999) Osteoporosis. Clinical guidelines for the prevention and treatment. London: RCP.

Shaywitz, S.E., Shaywitz, B.A. Pugh, K.R. *et al.* (1999) Effect of estrogen on brain activation patterns in postmenopausal women during working memory tasks. *JAMA* **281**, 1197–202.

Simon, J.A., Hsia, J., Cauley, J.A. *et al.* (2001) Postmenopausal hormone therapy and risk of stroke: the Heart and Estrogen-progestin Replacement Study (HERS). *Circulation* **103**, 638–42.

Smith, W., Mitchell, P. and Wang, J.J. (1997) Gender, oestrogen, hormone replacement and age-related macular degeneration: results from the Blue Mountains Eye Study. *Aust N Z J Ophthalmol* **25**, Suppl 1: S13–5.

Torgerson, D.J. and Bell-Syer, S.E. (2001) Hormone replacement therapy and prevention of nonvertebral fractures: a meta-analysis of randomized trials. *JAMA* **285**, 2891–7.

Wang, P.N., Liao, S.Q., Liu, R.S. *et al.* (2000) Effects of estrogen on cognition, mood, and cerebral blood flow in AD: a controlled study. *Neurology* **54**, 2061–6.

Chapter 5

Beresford, S.A., Weiss, N.S., Voigt, L.F. and McKnight, B. (1997) Risk of endometrial cancer in relation to use of oestrogen combined with cyclic progestagen therapy in post menopausal women. *Lancet* **349**, 458–61.

Brinton, L. and Hoover, R. (1993) Estrogen replacement therapy and endometrial cancer: unresolved issues. *Obstet Gynecol* **81**, 265–71.

Cobleigh, M.A. (1998) Hormone replacement therapy and nonhormonal control of menopausal symptoms in breast cancer survivors. *Cancer Treat Res* **94**, 209–30.

Dupont, W.D., Page, D.L., Parl, F.F. *et al.* (1999) Estrogen replacement therapy in women with a history of proliferative breast disease. *Cancer* **85**, 1277–83.

Grady, D., Gebretsadik, T., Kerlikowske, K., Ernster, V. and Petitti, D. (1995) Hormone replacement therapy and endometrial cancer risk: a meta-analysis. *Obstet Gynecol* **85**, 304–13.

Gutthann, S.P., Rodriguez, L.A., Castellsague, J. and Oliart, A.D. (1997) Hormone replacement therapy and risk of venous thromboembolism: population based case-control study. *Br Med J* **314**, 796–800.

Keeling, D. (1999) 'Hormone replacement therapy and thrombosis' in: S. Hope, M. Rees and J. Brockie (Eds) *Hormone Replacement Therapy: A Guide for Primary Care*. Oxford: Oxford Medical Publications, pp. 59–72.

Lowe, G., Woodward, M., Vessey, M. *et al.* (2000) Thrombotic variables and risk of idiopathic venous thromboembolism in women aged 45–64 years. Relationships to hormone replacement therapy. *Thromb Haemost* **83**, 530–5.

Pike, M.C., Peters, R.K., Cozen, W. *et al.* (1997) Estrogen-progestin replacement therapy and endometrial cancer. *J Natl Cancer Inst* 89, 1110–16.

Ross, R.K., Paganini-Hill, A., Wan, P.C. and Pike, M.C. (2000) Effect of hormone replacement therapy on breast cancer risk: estrogen versus estrogen plus progestin. *J Natl Cancer Inst* **92**, 328–32.

Royal College of Obstetricians and Gynaecologists (1999) Hormone replacement therapy and venous thromboembolism. Guideline No 19. London: RCOG Press.

Schairer, C., Lubin, J., Troisi, R. *et al.* (2000) Menopausal estrogen and estrogen-progestin replacement therapy and breast cancer risk. *JAMA* **283**, 485–91.

Van Baal, W.M., Emeis, J.J., van der Mooren, M.J. *et al.* (2000) Impaired procoagulant-anticoagulant balance during hormone replacement therapy? A randomised, placebo-controlled 12-week study. *Thromb Haemost* **83**, 29–34.

Weiderpass, E., Adami, H.O., Baron, J.A. *et al.* (1999) Risk of endometrial cancer following estrogen replacement with and without progestins. *J Natl Cancer Inst* **9**, 1131–7.

Weiderpass, E., Baron, J.A., Adami, H.O. *et al.* (1999) Low-potency oestrogen and risk of endometrial cancer: a case-control study. *Lancet* **353**, 1824–8.

Weiderpass, E., Persson, I., Adami, H.O. *et al.* (2000) Body size in different periods of life, diabetes mellitus, hypertension, and risk of postmenopausal endometrial cancer (Sweden). *Cancer Causes Control* **11**, 185–92.

Willis, D.B., Calle, E.E., Miracle-McMahill, H.L. and Heath, C.W. Jr. (1996) Estrogen replacement therapy and risk of fatal breast cancer in a prospective cohort of postmenopausal women in the United States. *Cancer Causes and Control* **7**, 449–57.

Chapter 6

Barrett-Connor, E. (1998) Hormone replacement therapy. *Br Med J* **317**, 457–61.

Bjorn, I. and Backsrom, T. (1999) Drug-related negative side-effects is a common reason for poor compliance in hormone replacement therapy. *Maturitas* **32**, 77–86.

Burger, H. and Davis, S. (1998) Should women be treated with testosterone? *Clin Endocrinol* **49**, 159–60.

Crook, D. (1999) Will the route of administration influence the potential cardiovascular benefits of HRT? *J Br Meno Soc* **5**, 35–9.

Davis, S.R. (1998) Androgens and the menopause *J Br Meno Soc* **4**, 87–95.

Ettinger, B., Pressman, A. and Bradley, C. (1998) Comparison of continuation of postmenopausal hormone replacement therapy: transdermal versus oral estrogen. *Menopause* **5**, 152–6.

Hammar, M., Christau, S., Nathorst-Boos, J., Rud, T. and Garre, K. (1998) A double-blind, randomised trial comparing the effects of tibolone and continuous combined hormone replacement therapy in postmenopausal women with menopausal symptoms. *Br J Obstet Gynaecol* **105**, 904–11.

Heikkinen, J.E., Vaheri, R.T., Ahomaki, S.M. *et al.* (2000) Optimizing continuous-combined hormone replacement therapy for postmenopausal women: a comparison of six different treatment regimens. *Am J Obstet Gynecol* **182**, 560–7.

Hill, D.A., Weiss, N.S. and LaCroix, A.Z. (2000) Adherence to postmenopausal hormone therapy during the year after the initial prescription: a population-based study. *Am J Obstet Gynecol* **182**, 270–6.

Loprinzi, C.L., Michalak, J.C. and Quella, S.K. *et al.* (1994) Megestrol acetate for the prevention of hot flashes. *N Engl J Med* **331**, 347–52.

Miller, K.K. (2001) Androgen deficiency in women. *J Clin Endocrinol Metab* **86**, 2395–401.

Monthly Index of Medical Specialities. London: Haymarket Medical Ltd.

Notelovtiz, M., Lenihan, J.P., McDermott, L. *et al.* (2000) Initial 17ß-estradiol dose for treating vasomotor symptoms. *Am J Obstet Gynecol* **95**, 726–31.

Rees, M.C. (2000) The endometrium and hormone replacement: safety and bleeding *J Br Meno Soc Suppl* **1**, S6–9.

Rees, M. C. and Purdie, D.W. (Eds) (1999) *Management of the Menopause*. Marlow: BMS Publications.

Sulak, P.J., Caubel, P. and Lane, R. (1999) Efficacy and safety of a constant-estrogen, pulsed-progestin regimen in hormone replacement therapy. *Int J Fertil Womens Med* **44**, 286–96.

Suvanto-Luukkonen, E., Sundstrom, H., Penttinen, J. and Kauppila, A. (1998) Lipid effects of an intrauterine levonorgestrel device or oral vs. vaginal natural progesterone in post-menopausal women treated with percutaneous estradiol. *Arch Gynecol Obstet* **261**, 201–8.

Vessey, M.P., Villard-Mackintosh, L., McPherson, K., Coulter, A. and Yeates, D. (1992) The epidemiology of hysterectomy: findings in a large cohort study. *Br J Obstet Gynaecol* **99**, 402–7.

Watkinson, A.C. (2001) The pharmacokinetics of drug delivery systems in hormone replacement therapy. *J Br Meno Soc* **7**, 105–8.

Chapter 7

Affinito, P., Sorrentino, C., Farace, M.J. *et al.* (1996) Effects of thyroxine therapy on bone metabolism in postmenopausal women with hypothyroidism. *Acta Obstet Gynecol Scand* **75**, 843–8.

Abbasi, F., Krumholz, A., Kittner, S.J. and Langenberg, P. (1999) Effects of menopause on seizures in women with epilepsy. *Epilepsia* **40**, 205–10.

Blanchet, P.J., Fang, J., Hyland, K., Arnold, L.A., Mouradian, M.M. and Chase, T.N. (1999) Short-term effects of high-dose 17beta-estradiol in postmenopausal PD patients: a crossover study. *Neurology* **53**, 91–5.

Cummings, S.R., Nevitt, M.C., Browner, W.S. *et al.* (1995) Risk factors for hip fracture in white women. Study of Osteoporotic Fractures. Research Group. *N Engl J Med* **332**, 767–73.

De-Valk-de-Roo, G.W., Stehouwer, C.D., Meijer, P. *et al.* (1999) Both raloxifene and estrogen reduce major cardiovascular risk factors in healthy post menopausal women: a two-year, placebo-controlled study. *Arterioscler Thromb Vasc Biol* **12**, 2993–3000.

Dupont, W.D., Page, D.L., Parl, F.F. *et al.* (1999). Estrogen replacement therapy in women with a history of proliferative breast disease. *Cancer* **85**, 1277–83.

Feldkamp, J., Becker, A., Witte, O.W., Scharff, D., Scherbaum, W.A. (2000) Long-term anticonvulsant therapy leads to low bone mineral density – evidence for direct drug effects of phenytoin and carbamazepine on human osteoblast-like cells. *Exp Clin Endocrinol Diabetes* **108**, 37–43.

Green, P.S. and Simpkins, J.W. (2000) Neuroprotective effects of estrogens: potential mechanisms of action. *Int J Dev Neurosci* **18**, 347–58.

Hall, G.M., Daniels, M., Huskisson, E.C. and Spector, T.D. (1994) A randomised controlled trial of the effect of hormone replacement therapy on disease activity in postmenopausal rheumatoid arthritis. *Ann. Rheum Dis* **53**, 112–6.

Hallengren, B., Elmstahl, B., Berglund, J. *et al.* (1999) No increase in fracture incidence in patients treated for thyrotoxicosis in Malmo during 1970–74. A 20-year population-based follow-up. *J Intern Med* **246**, 139–44.

Harden, C.L., Pulver, M.C., Ravdin, L. and Jacobs, A.R. (1999) The effect of menopause and perimenopause on the course of epilepsy. *Epilepsia* **40**, 1402–7.

Jodar, E., Munoz-Torres, M., Escobar-Jimenez, F., Quesada-Charneco, M. and Lund del Castillo, J.D. (1997) Bone loss in hyperthyroid patients and in former hyperthyroid patients controlled on medical therapy: influence of aetiology and menopause. *Clin Endocrinol (Oxf)* **47**, 279–85.

Koepsell, T.D., Dugowsen, C.E., Nelson, J.L., Voight, L.F. and Daling, J.R. (1994) Non-contraceptive hormones and the risk of rheumatoid arthritis in menopausal women. *Int J Epidemiol* **23**, 1248–55.

Kreidstein, S., Urowitz, M.B., Gladman, D.D. and Gough, J. (1997) Hormone replacement therapy in systemic lupus erythematosus. *J Rheumatol* **24**, 2149–52.

MacGregor, E.A. (1997) Menstruation, sex hormones, and migraine. *Neurol Clin* **15**, 125–41.

Persson, I., Yuen, J., Bergkvist, L., Schairer, C. (1996) Cancer incidence and mortality in women receiving estrogen and estrogen-progestin replacement therapy-long-term follow-up of a Swedish cohort. *Int J Cancer* **67**, 327–32.

Ramsey-Goldman, R., Dunn, J.E., Dunlop, D.D. *et al.* (1999) Increased risk of fracture in patients receiving solid organ transplants. *J Bone Miner Res* **14**, 456–63.

Ramsey-Goldman, R., Dunn, J.E., Huang, C.F. *et al.* (1999). Frequency of fractures in women with systemic lupus erythematosus: comparison with United States population data. *Arthritis Rheum* **42**, 882–90.

Rodriguez, C., Patel, A.V., Calle, E.E., Jacob, E.J. and Thun, M.J. (2001) Estrogen replacement therapy and ovarian cancer mortality in a large prospective study of US women. *JAMA* **285**, 1460–65.

Rohan, T.E. and Miller, A.B. (1999) Hormone replacement therapy and risk of benign proliferative epithelial disorders of the breast. *Eur J Cancer Prev* **8**, 123–30.

Rosciszewska, D. (1986) Menopause in women and its effects on women. *Neurol Neurochir Polska* **12**, 315–19.

Seed, M. (1999) Hormone replacement therapy and cardiovascular disease. *Curr Opin Lipidol* **10**, 581–7.

Smith, M.A., Fine, J.A., Barnhill, R.L. and Berwick, M. (1998) Hormonal and reproductive influences and risk of melanoma in women. *Int J Epidemiol* **27**, 751–7.

Stehman-Breen, C.O., Gillen, D. and Gipson, D. (1999) Prescription of hormone replacement therapy in postmenopausal women with renal failure. *Kidney Int* **56**, 2243–7.

Chapter 8

Andersson, K., Pedersen, A.T., Mattsson, L.A. and Milsom, I. (1998) Swedish gynecologists' and general practitioners' views on the climacteric period: knowledge, attitudes and management strategies. *Acta Obstet Gynecol Scand* **77**, 909–16.

Archer, D.F., Lobo, R.A., Land, H.F. and Pickar, J.H. (1999) A comparative study of transvaginal uterine ultrasound and endometrial biopsy for evaluating the endometrium of postmenopausal women taking hormone replacement therapy. *Menopause* **6**, 201–8.

Bastian, L., Couchman, G., Rimer, B.K. et al. (1998) Promoting informed decision making: hormone replacement therapy. *Cancer Treat Res* **97**, 129–47.

Bradley, C. (1999) Compliance with drug therapy. *Prescribers' Journal* **39**, 44–50.

Greendale, G.A., Reboussin, B.A. and Sie, A. *et al.* (1999) Effects of estrogen and estrogen-progestin on mammographic parenchymal density. Postmenopausal Estrogen/Progestin Interventions (PEPI) Investigators. *Ann Intern Med* **130**, 262–9.

Harris, T.J., Cook, D.G., Wicks, P.D. and Cappuccio, F.P. (1999) Ethnic differences in use of hormone replacement therapy: community based survey. *Br Med J* **319**, 610–1.

Harrison-Woolrych, M. (2001) Breast and pelvic examination in women taking hormone replacement therapy. *J Br Meno Soc* **7**, 103.

Hope, S. and Rees, M.C. (1995) Why do British women start and stop hormone replacement therapy? *J Br Meno Soc* **1**, 26–7.

Hope, S., Wager, E. and Rees, M.C. (1998) Survey of British women's views on the menopause and HRT. *J Br Meno Soc* **4**, 33–6.

Isaacs, A.J., Britton, A.R. and McPherson, K. (1997) Why do women doctors in the UK take hormone replacement therapy? *J Epidemiol Community Health* **51**, 373–7.

Jick, H., Jick, S., Meyers M. W. and Vasilakis, C. (1996) Risk of acute myocardial infarction and low-dose combined oral contraceptives. *Lancet* **347**, 627–8.

Lindgren, R., Mattsson, L.A., Andersson, K. *et al.* (1999) Transvaginal ultra-sonography and endometrial histology in peri- and postmenopausal women on hormone replacement therapy. *Br J Obstet Gynaecol* **106**, 421–6.

Litherland, J.C., Stallard, S., Hole, D. and Cordiner, C. (1999) The effect of hormone replacement therapy on the sensitivity of screening mammograms. *Clin Radiol* **54**, 285–8.

Lundstrom, E., Wilczek, B., von Palffy, Z., Soderqvist, G. and von Schoultz, B. (1999) Mammographic breast density during hormone replacement therapy: differences according to treatment. *Am J Obstet Gynecol* **181**, 348–52.

North American Menopause Society (1998) Achieving long-term continuance of menopausal ERT/HRT: consensus opinion of the North American Menopause Society. *Menopause* **5**, 69–76.

Nybo Andersen, A.-M., Wohlfahrt, J., Christens, P., Olsen, J. and Melbye, M. (2000) Maternal age and fetal loss: population based register linkage study. *Br Med J* **320**, 1708–12.

Page, C. and Glasier, A. (2000) 'Monitoring of women on hormone replacement therapy: what should we be doing?' In: J.W. Studd (Ed.) *The Management of the Menopause*. Carnforth, UK: Parthenon Publishing, p. 49–58.

Sterns, E.E. and Zee, B. (2000) Mammographic density changes in perimenopausal and postmenopausal women: is effect of hormone replacement therapy predictable? *Breast Cancer Res Treat* **59**, 125–32.

Wordsworth, J. (1999) Contraception at the perimenopause. *J Br Meno Soc* **4**, 123–4.

Chapter 9

Black, D.M., Cummings, SR., Karpf, D.B. *et al.* (1996) Randomised trial of effect of alendronate on risk of fracture in women with existing vertebral fractures. *Lancet* **348**, 1535–41.

Bone, H.G., Greenspan, S.L., McKeever, C. *et al.* (2000) Alendronate and estrogen effects in postmenopausal women with low bone mineral density. Alendronate/Estrogen Study Group. *J Clin Endocrinol Metab* **85**, 720–6.

Chapuy, M.C., Arlot, M.E., Duboeuf, F. *et al.* (1992) Vitamin D3 and calcium to prevent hip fractures in elderly women. *N Engl J Med* **327**, 1637–42.

Cosman, F. and Lindsay, R. (1998) Is parathyroid hormone a therapeutic option for osteoporosis: a review of the clinical evidence. *Calcif Int* **62**, 475–80.

Cumming, R.G. and Nevitt, M.C. (1997) Calcium for the prevention of osteoporotic fractures in postmenopausal women. *J Bone Miner Res* **12**, 1321–9.

Davies, M. (1998) Non HRT options for the treatment of osteoporosis. *J Br Meno Soc* **4**, 96–101.

Delmas, P.D., Bjarnason, N.H., Mitlak, B.H. *et al.* (1997) Effects of raloxifene on bone mineral density, serum cholesterol concentrations, and uterine endometrium in postmenopausal women. *N Engl J Med* **337**, 1641–7.

DTB (1999) Raloxifene to prevent postmenopausal osteoporosis. *Drug and Therapeutics Bulletin* **37**, 33–6.

Ettinger, B., Black, D.M., Mitlak, B.H. *et al.* (1999) Reduction of vertebral fracture risk in postmenopausal women treated with raloxifene. Results from a 3-year randomized clinical trial. *JAMA* **282**, 637–45.

Harris, S.T., Watts, N.B., Genant, H.K. *et al.* (1999) Effects of risedronate treatment on vertebral and nonvertebral fractures in women with postmenopausal osteoporosis: a randomized controlled trial. Vertebral Efficacy With Risedronate Therapy (VERT) Study Group. *JAMA* **282**, 1344–52.

Heath, D.A., Bullivant, B.G., Boiven, C. and Balena, R. (2000) The effects of cyclical etidronate on early postmenopausal bone loss: an open, randomized controlled study. *J Clin Densitom* **3**, 27–33.

Heikinheimo, R.J., Inkovaara, J.A., Harju, E.J. *et al.* (1992) Annual injection of vitamin D and fractures of aged bones. *Calcif Tissue Int* **51**, 105–10.

Liberman, U.A., Weiss, S.R., Broll, J. *et al.* (1995) Effect of oral alendronate on bone mineral density and the incidence of fractures in postmenopausal osteoporosis. *N Engl J Med* **333**, 1437–43.

Overgaard, K., Hansen, M.A., Jensen, S.B. and Christiansen, C. (1992) Effect of salcatonin given intranasally on bone mass and fracture rates in established osteoporosis: a dose-response study. *Br Med J* **305**, 556–61.

Reginster, J., Minne, H.W., Sorensen, O.H. *et al.* (2000) Randomized trial of the effects of risedronate on vertebral fractures in women with established postmenopausal osteoporosis. Vertebral Efficacy with Risedronate Therapy (VERT) Study Group. *Osteoporos Int* **11**, 83–91.

Reid, D.M., Hughes, R.A., Laan, R.F. *et al.* (2000) Efficacy and safety of daily risedronate in the treatment of corticosteroid-induced osteoporosis in men and women: a randomized trial. European Corticosteroid-Induced Osteoporosis Treatment Study. *J Bone Miner Res* **15**, 1006–13.

Storm, T., Thamsborg, G., Steiniche, T., Genant, H.K. and Sorensen, O.H. (1990) Effect of intermittent cyclical etidronate therapy on bone mass and fracture rate in women with postmenopausal osteoporosis. *N Engl J Med* **322**, 1265–71.

Tilyard, M.W., Spears, G.F., Thomson, J. and Dovey, S. (1992) Treatment of postmenopausal osteoporosis with calcitriol or calcium. *N Engl J Med* **326**, 357–62.

Wimalawansa, S.J. (1998). A four-year randomized controlled trial of hormone replacement and bisphosphonate, alone or in combination, in women with postmenopausal osteoporosis. *Am J Med* **104**, 219–26.

Woo, T. and Adachi, J.D. (2001) Role of bisphosphonates and calcitonin in the prevention and treatment of osteoporosis. *Best Pract Res Clin Rheumatol* **15**, 469–81.

Chapter 10

Baulieu, E.E., Thomas, G., Legrain, S. *et al.* (2000) Dehydroepiandrosterone (DHEA), DHEA sulfate, and aging: contribution of the DHEAge Study to a sociobiomedical issue. *Proc Nat Acad Sci USA* **97**, 4279–84.

DTB (2001) 'Natural' progesterone creams for postmenopausal women. *Drug Ther Bull* **39**, 10–11.

Ernst, E. (1999) Herbal remedies as a treatment of some frequent symptoms during menopause. *J Br Meno Soc* **5**, 117–20.

Hinson, J.P. and Raven, P.W. (1999) DHEA deficiency syndrome: a new term for old age? *J Endocrinol* **163**, 1–5.

Knight, D.C., Howes, J.B., Eden, J.A. and Howes, L.G. (2001) Effects on menopausal symptoms and acceptability of isoflavone-containing soy powder dietary supplementation. *Climacteric* **4**, 13–18.

McKenna, D.J., Jones, K., Humphrey, S. and Hughes, K. (2001) Black cohosh: efficacy, safety, and use in clinical and preclinical applications. *Altern Ther Health Med* **7**, 93–100.

Quella, S.K., Loprinzi, C.L., Barton, D.L. *et al.* (2000) Evaluation of soy phytoestrogens for the treatment of hot flushes in breast cancer survivors: A North Central Cancer Treatment Group Trial. *J Clin Oncol* **18**, 1068–74.

Simons, L.A., von Konigsmark, M., Simons, J. and Celermajer, D.S. (2000) Phytoestrogens do not influence lipoprotein levels or endothelial function in healthy, postmenopausal women. *Am J Cardiol* **85**, 1297–301.

Washburn, S., Burke, G.L., Morgan, T. and Anthony, M. (1999) Effect of soy protein supplementation on serum lipoproteins, blood pressure, and menopausal symptoms in perimenopausal women. *Menopause* **6**, 7–13.

Wren, B.G., McFarland, K. and Edwards, L. (1999) Micronised transdermal progesterone and endometrial response. *Lancet* **354**, 1447–8.

Index